ALSO BY DAHLIA ABRAHAM-KLEIN

Silk Road Vegetarian:
Vegan, Vegetarian and Gluten Free Recipes for the Mindful Cook
[Vegetarian Cookbook, 101 Recipes]

Spiritual Kneading through the Jewish Months:
Building the Sacred through Challah

Necessary Mourning:
Healing the Loss of a Parent through Jewish Ritual

CARAVAN *of* HOPE

A Bukharan Woman's Journey to Freedom

DAHLIA ABRAHAM-KLEIN

SHAMASHI PRESS
NEW YORK

CARAVAN OF HOPE:
A Bukharan Woman's Journey to Freedom
by Dahlia Abraham-Klein

Library of Congress Control Number: 2023905158

Cover and design: Tami Boyce (tamiboyce.com)
Publisher: Shamashi Press
Editor: Katherine Factor

ISBN: 979-8-218-17848-2

1. BIOGRAPHY & AUTOBIOGRAPHY / Cultural, Ethnic & Regional / Asian & Asian American 2. BIOGRAPHY & AUTOBIOGRAPHY / Historical 3. BIOGRAPHY & AUTOBIOGRAPHY / Women

First Edition 10 9 8 7 6 5 4 3 2 1
Printed in the United States

DEDICATION

For our Bibish, Dora Abraham, who lived for her family.
For her sacrifice and endurance, we, her children, grandchildren,
and great-grandchildren, are free to live the life she wanted for us—
Jewish, educated, professional, and thriving.

Minsk
BELARUS
Homyel
Dnieper
Kiev
Dnieper
UKRAINE
Donets'k
Sea of
Azov
Rostov
Don
Don
Sevastopol
Novorossiysk
Black Sea
Moscow
Nizhniy
Novgorod
Volga
Volga
Kazan'
Samara
Saratov
Volga
Oral
Volgograd
Zhayyq
Astrakhan'
Atyraū
Caspian
Sea
Aqtaū
Sokhumi
Groznyy
Bat'umi
GEORGIA
Trabzon
Tbilisi
TURKEY
ARMENIA
Yerevan
AZERBAIJAN
Sumqayit
Xandäni
Baku
Türkmenbasy
Lake
Van
Naxçivan
Tabriz
Lake
Lirmia
Balkanabat
Gyzylarbat
Aleppo
Euphrates
Mosul
SYRIA
Arbil
Tigris
Tehran
RDAN
SAUDI
IRAQ
Baghdad
IRAN

CAUCASUS AND CENTRAL ASIA
RUSSIA
Yekaterinburg
Chelyabinsk
Petropavlovsk
Pavlodar
Qostanay
Astana
Semey
Öskemen
Qaraghandy
KAZAKHSTAN
Saryshaghan
Lake Balkhash
Qyzylorda
Almaty
Aral Sea
Taraz
Talas
Bishkek
UZBEKISTAN
Shymkent
KYRGYZSTAN
Nukus
Namangan
Andijon
Dasoguz
Tashkent
Osh
Urganch
Kashi
Navoiy
Jizzax
Khujand
CH
Buxoro
Samarqand
TAJIKISTAN
Turkmenabat
Qarshi
Dushanbe
TURKMENISTAN
Khorugh
shgabat
Mary
Termiz
PAKISTAN
Mashhad
Kabul
Gusgy
Islamabad
INDIA
AFGHANISTAN
Ob
Irtysh
Indus

FOREWORD

The germination for this book was a simple question: "Where are you from?"

This question prompted my mother, Zina Abraham, born in 1933 in a Russian prison, to tell her story to the Bal Harbour sisterhood. It was a telling of the unknown stories of a civilization that mainly was uneducated, running for their lives with no time nor the wherewithal to write their stories down. This project – the re-telling of these stories – has been a challenging but worthy effort, and I hope this can honor the perseverance of those Central Asian Jews whose spirit deserves more of a voice.

My mother's vivid life—lived with hope and grace despite all odds—also became a personal journey in the making of the book. As we compiled first-person interviews, photographs, and family stories, not only did the family's perseverance become apparent, it also became evident that few stories existed for the public about Central Asian Jews, collectively known as "Bukharan Jews." The Emirate of Bukhara was the last emirate of the Mangit dynasty of Uzbeks from 1785 to 1920. The term "Bukharan" was adopted due to this emirate coining the collective name of the peoples that hailed from Uzbekistan, Tajikistan, Turkmenistan, and Kazakhstan as Bukharan's.

Central Asia stretches from the Caspian Sea in the west to China and Mongolia in the east and from Afghanistan and Iran in the south to Russia in the north. The region consists of the former Soviet republics, colloquially referred to as "the stans." The countries all have names ending with the Persian suffix "stan," meaning "land of," since Iranian non-Persian tribes in antiquity had populated these countries.

The Central Asian Jews' oral tradition states that their ancestors came from Babylon and moved on to Persia. My family's migration on my father's side took place in the 18th-19th century when the entire Jewish community of Mashhad was compelled to accept Shi'i Islam in 1839. Some forced converts were able to flee eastward, my family included, returning to a more open practice of Judaism in Afghanistan. Others, like my grandmother from my mother's side, likely arrived in the 13th-14th century, settling in Bukhara.

The "Mizrachi Jews"—also known as "Eastern Jews"— were mostly uneducated, as only an informal Jewish education was available. If any secular education was available, it was rudimentary math. Consequently, there is so little written history, let alone an account of Central Asian Jews. Most Jewish history begins with World War II in Europe, but a vast swath of Jews underwent forced conversions, pogroms, murders, rape, and kidnapping that preceded Europe's persecution. Central Asia Jewish history was a precursor to what was to come.

What separated Mizrachi Jews from the rest of world Jewry is that they underwent multigenerational trauma without even knowing it. It was just life. To work, lose, and move. *Constantly.* For hundreds of years. They were so busy moving and escaping persecution that lamenting the circumstances did not exist. Consequently, living the merchant's life, no one had time to record their own story. No one had time to feel pity for themselves, besetting a layer of stoicism upon them.

My grandmother Dora's formative years in the early 1900s were under the Golden Age of Bukharan Jewry, which under the Russian protectorate, enjoyed personal liberties, formal education, and economic opportunities. My great-grandfather Moshe—Dora's father—made vast fortunes traveling and trading with Moscow in gold and diamonds. This all came to a grinding halt when the Bolshevik Revolution of 1917 brought the Red Army to Central Asia in 1920. While the last Emir was removed from office, Bukhara maintained relative autonomy under the Bukharan People's Soviet Republic until 1924. At that point, it became part of the Soviet Socialist Republic of Uzbekistan, with Tashkent developing into its principal city. After a few years of looking favorably upon the Jews for supporting the Soviet takeover, the Stalinist regime began eradicating Judaism and religion in general from its empire. This was when purgatory began for my grandmother. Her father was taken to a labor camp in Siberia, where he perished. The family fortune was confiscated, and the family once again became refugees.

Underneath all the loss is a story of survival and a deep commitment to a better life. Every move was progress towards that unwavering goal.

I've become a biographer to my parents' lives. I owe it to them and my ancestors to share this story of a resolute but quiet, ongoing belief in hope. To stand against illiteracy, against oppression. I've been granted the education to chronicle their lives.

This story is my mother's history of an ancient enclave of Jews that lived in the region due to the dispersion of our peoples after the destruction of the Holy Temple in Jerusalem in 586 BCE. It spans lands from Central Asia to America and dissolves boundaries through the commonality of perseverance and hope. It shows a force for life, better circumstances, and hope that conquers all odds for family—and into Jewish perpetuity.

In writing this book as creative non-fiction, I've done my best to verify factual aspects of the memories and stories and have relied on my family recollections for details that I could not confirm. I've done my best to weave this narrative into a tapestry summing it up as a Caravan of Hope.

Dahlia Abraham-Klein
New York, 2023

CONTENTS

TIMELINE

1906: Birth of Dora Yugadayev, in Kokand, Uzbek (now Uzbekistan), born to Bracha and Moshe Yugadayev.

1917-1923: The Russian Revolution. A period of political and social revolution in the former Russian Empire began during the First World War; Russia abolished its monarchy and adopted a socialist form of government following two successive revolutions and a bloody civil war.

1919: Anglo-Afghan war ends. Afghan independence sparked a fierce nationalism.

1919-1923: King Amanullah attempted to introduce significant reforms, including coeducational schools, and the unveiling of women, via a new constitution. Such moves angered the conservatives, who drove him from his throne. Afghan Jews had intense hostility towards the government's effort to bring Jewish children to their public schools to indoctrinate them with Muslim beliefs. Their resolve was profoundly ingrained, and family structure was emphasized.

1920: Bukhara Operation: many Bukharan Jews fled to the West. The route they undertook went through Afghanistan, as the neighboring country had many opportunities.

1920-1930: Hundreds of Bukharan Jews fled Bolshevism and settled in Afghanistan.

1929-1933: King Muhammad Nadir Shah formulated a more conservative constitution in 1931 to please Muslim co-religionists. The economy grew as small businesses developed.

1929-1953: Josef Stalin in power as General Secretary of the Communist Party in the Soviet Union.

1929: Dora's father, Moshe Yugadayev, is taken to a Siberian work camp to die after being targeted for wealth.

1930-1940: Rising nationalist desire in Afghanistan to drive Jews and other non-Muslims from the financial sector leads to a new-found surge in Jewish edicts.

1932: Train station meeting between Hasid Shamash and Shura Yugadayev Samuel prompted Shura to introduce him to her sister, Dora. Marriage between Hasid and Dora in Kokand. Dora is 26 years old. Hasid is smuggled from Kokand to Herat, Afghanistan, to avoid persecution for diamonds.

1933: Dora is imprisoned in the Soviet Union at three months pregnant. Jewish edicts are enforced in Afghanistan. Jews are only permitted to live in specific cities. Dora gives birth to Zina Shamash in prison. They are released from prison when Zina is six months old. Soviet Jews and Bukharan's in Afghanistan implore the Board of Deputy of British Jews' permission for the refugees to remain free in the northern Afghan towns until the rest of their families arrive from the Soviet Union.

1934: Dora and Zina are released from prison and make the arduous journey from Soviet Uzbek to Herat, Afghanistan by horse.

1933-1973: King Muhammad Zahir Shah is open to democracy. Though he became King because his father was assassinated, he desperately sought to improve the country on the world stage by modernizing its infrastructure and technology. He also signed formal accords with Germany, and brought hundreds of Germans from various professions to Afghanistan. Germany felt that a German presence in Central Asia would advance Nazi interests, intimidating Britain and the Soviet Union (1936-1941).

1936: Birth of second Shamash daughter, Zipora, in Herat, Afghanistan.

1938: Birth of the third Shamash daughter, Yafa, in Kabul, Afghanistan.

1939: Birth of the first son, Moshe, in Kabul, Afghanistan.

1940: Birth of fourth daughter, Rosa, in Kabul, Afghanistan.

1945: Birth of fifth daughter, Tamar, in Kabul, Afghanistan.

1946: Birth of sixth daughter, Hanna, in Kabul, Afghanistan.

1948: Formation of the State of Israel. When the State of Israel was established, the Jewish community saw it as a fulfillment of biblical prophecy to return to their birthright land. Most left as soon as legal emigration was authorized.

1949: The Shamash family boards the first bus of families to leave Kabul and immigrate to Israel. Zina is 16 years old.

1951: Bracha, seventh daughter of Dora and Hasid, is born in Israel and named after her mother.

1953: Zina, 20 years old, and Yehuda Abraham marry in Israel and move to Bombay, India. The family's last name changes from Shamash to Abraham.

1953: Zina and Yehuda Abraham's first daughter, Shirley, is born in India.

1956: Yehuda, Zina, and Shirley move to Rego Park, New York.

1957: Zina and Yehuda Abraham first son, Gideon, is born in New York.

1960s: Family gem business opens satellite offices in Thailand, Japan, India, Italy, Switzerland, Hong Kong, and Israel.

1961: Zina and Yehuda Abraham second son, Jackie, is born in New York.

1963: A grand birthday celebration in Tel Aviv for Agajan and Chana Abramoff, grandparents of Zina, where the family dedicates a Sefer Torah in honor of Zina's grandfather's one-hundred-year birthday and seventieth wedding anniversary.

1966: Dora travels to Uzbekistan to visit with her family who she has not seen in thirty years.

1969: Zina and Yehuda Abraham second daughter, Dahlia, is born in New York.

1970s: Yehuda and his brother Mayer become active members of the Sephardic Congregation of Queens, alternating between President and Vice President. They hire Rabbi Shalom Hecht to lead the congregation.

1970s: Yehuda and Mayer set up the first synagogue in the Bangkok business district in their home/office, *Even Chen*, which means warm stone, an ode to their gem business.

1980s: Zina and Yehuda are active philanthropists in the Jewish community and are recognized by the United Jewish Appeal as outstanding leaders in their community. At the request of the Lubavitcher Rebbe, Mayer and Yehuda build a *mikvah* in Bangkok called *Mikvah Rachel*, after their beloved mother.

1993: Dora passes away and is buried in Israel next to her mother, Bracha.

2010s: Torah scrolls from Zina's grandparents are located in Israel, restored and donated to Even Chen in Bangkok, and the second scroll to a synagogue in Hong Kong.

2014: Yehuda passes and is buried in Israel after a marriage of over fifty-five years.

2015: Zina moves to Miami.

2017: Bukharan Night on February 2.

BAL HARBOUR SISTERHOOD

At one of the most popular Chabad-run shuls in Surfside, Florida, over one hundred sisterhood members gathered for *parsha*[1] studies on a Saturday to hear Rebbitzen Chani Lipskar. The synagogue has thousands of members, and has been recognized by *Newsweek* as a most vibrant congregation with a mission of inclusivity.

Zina Abraham, a member since moving to Florida in 2015, read the mission as she entered, "A home away from home, a gathering place where unity is paramount. We are here for you; welcome to the family."

She took her seat, reflecting on how the remarkable origins of the congregation started with Rabbi Sholom Lipskar gathering local Jews in hotel rooms and storefronts despite the community

---

1 *Parsha (Hebrew)*- Jewish weekly Torah portion

refusing a Jewish presence. To Zina, this reminded her of her family history, of society's dismissal of her culture. Yet the tenets of the shul resonated with her- 'To love every Jew as one loves himself and to permeate that love with Acts of Kindness, Mitzvot, Torah Study, and Prayer' -reflected what could just as easily be Zina's own life of homemaking and cultural contributions.

As she sat down, Zina contemplated how the shul's sisterhood regularly participated in the luncheons and fundraising events that provide a venue and platform for women to reach out to each other. But Zina had a special relationship with Rabbi Sholom Lipskar and his wife, Rebbitzen Chani Lipskar.

"Where are you from?" the Rebbetzin asked some of the members.

When it was Zina's turn, she sat up with pride, sharing, "I was born in Bukhara and raised in Afghanistan, but my life has taken me across several continents. So I'm not sure I come from one place."

The sisters shuffled in their seats, unsure of what Bukhara meant but aware of a story unfolding. Zina's spirit filled the room. Her independence and agency were apparent; it was clear that she had taken charge of her eventful life. They listened to this elegant, graceful woman sharing anecdotes about her remarkable family and unusual life.

"My life can be divided into chapters. First are the unusual circumstances of how my parents met, then the frightening trials my mother went through with a new baby just after her marriage."

The crowd looked at each other, alerted to a new life, an unknown story, and a strong woman. "We want to hear more!" was the resounding response.

"I was raised in Afghanistan with no education and no freedom as a young girl. I almost died from diphtheria as a child because I was not allowed into a hospital as a girl. The only real education I received was when I lived in Pakistan for a year. That was *'Gan Eden'* compared to Afghanistan. I had to leave Pakistan because it was unsafe for Jews when the Muslims started to take over. When the State of Israel was born, I told my parents that I wanted to go. My father agreed, but my mother did not. She said, 'If you are going, we are all going.' And so we left. My mother took my sisters and brother and me by bus to Tehran to reach the new Jewish state. And that is just the beginning of my life."

A friend next to her interrupted— "Even though I am your neighbor, I did not realize how rich your past was . . ."

"I have an idea," Rebbetzin Chani said, "How would you like to host a Bukharan event for the community? We could all come in Bukharan costume, help make the food and you could share more of your story, so we can learn more about this ancient community in the middle of Asia." Everyone agreed, excited and in awe of Zina's life.

Zina invited the Rebbetzin over. "Chani, come to my home. I'll show you the photographs of my family. We will let the photos talk while I walk you through a hundred years and many, many countries."

Chani came over to her seat and extended her hand, "It would be my honor." Zina felt a buzzing warmth rising in the room.

Zina replied to the congregation, "But first, if you must know, I was born in a Russian prison."

CHAPTER 2

ESCAPE TO KOKAND

"Where are you traveling to?" the bellow of an Afghani policeman's voice cut through the dust-laden open-air train station. A man, and a woman in a blue *chadaree*[1], waited with their two toddlers for a train. A train ride that meant more freedom and safety for the family.

The woman's eyes darted nervously while the children shifted from foot to foot, bored and impatient in the heat. Shura held their hands tightly so they wouldn't jump off the short platform onto the tracks to kick up the pebbles. She clenched the hands of her son and daughter harder; her nerves accelerated, but she kept her face still as a frozen pond, eyes down. Being noticed now might single them out.

---

1 *Chadaree*– a large piece of cloth that is wrapped around the head and upper body leaving only the face exposed, worn especially by Muslim women.

It was 1932 at a small train station in Mazar, Afghanistan, riddled with desert winds. Shura felt sure that she and Ari, her husband, stood out and she felt targeted. She was a tall, broad-bodied brunette with warm blue eyes in tired drooping eyelids. She was also unmistakably Jewish. In a country where dress indicated identity and status, Afghan Muslim women were set apart by white *chadaree* while Jewish women donned exclusively blue fabrics.

Bukharan Jews fled Kokand when the Russian Empire annexed it, seeking better economic and religious freedoms. Kokand is a city in the Fergana Region in eastern Uzbekistan, at the southwestern edge of the Fergana Valley. Afghanistan sits south of Uzbekistan. Initially, the Russians sought the loyalty of the Bukharan Jews as they saw the Jews as their only friends among the newly conquered populations. This friendship was due to years of close trade between Jewish and Russian merchants. Russia did not restrict Jewish autonomy and aided the Bukharan's in becoming a powerful trading class within Central Asia and the Russian Empire.

Rather quickly, this came to an end when the Muslim military commander of Bukhara- the Emir, subjugated the Jewish population, blaming them for the Russian invasion. Persecution and money extortion led to an exodus of Jews from Bukhara to other Turkistan cities.

Simultaneously, the King, Muhammad Nadir Shah, instituted policies that favored *ethnic* Afghans and granted capital exclusively to this group. The economy shifted from one reliant on mercantilism to one reliant on a central bank—the Bank-e-Millie. And while its foremost goals had been to counteract the global depression and halt the falling Afghan currency, the measures effectively pushed Jewish citizens to the far fringes of the economy. Jews became a separate category from Afghans and came to be considered *foreign* influences, despite many Jews holding Afghan citizenship. In effect, Jewish citizens were lumped in with Jewish Soviet refugees and were considered agents of communism.

Then in the early 1930s, due to Stalin's genocidal excesses, more Soviet refugees were pushed to Afghanistan's northern border. Shura and Ari were part of this package of Bukharan Jews and Soviet refugees, who were a source of great concern for the Afghan government. Soviet Jewish refugees were considered very dangerous and potentially Soviet agents. Afghan suspicion then extended to the local Jewish population.

The Afghan economy sought to protect itself through a monopolization system. Much of the Jewish community's discrimination was directed through the Ministry of National Economy and the Afghan National Bank. This strategy was adopted ostensibly to limit Soviet influence in Afghanistan and benefit the Pashtun majority.

"We are going to Herat," Ari lied in a terse response to hide his Russian accent. It would have been dicey to expose that they were going to a Soviet protectorate, further putting them under suspicion as Soviet spies. Choosing a major city in western Afghanistan wouldn't cause alarm. His voice conveyed more strength than he felt. In truth, the family was planning to visit Shura's family in Kokand, an annex of Southern Russia, while Ari would continue trade with Russia. Shura held her breath, as her sweaty hands cupped the hands of her son and daughter. Her heart thumped as she waited for the policeman to respond.

The police officer silently walked them to the platform for the Herat-bound train. He nodded his head, waved his hand, wished them safe travels, and left. It wasn't until he was completely out of sight that Shura and Ari could breathe fully again.

CHAPTER 3

SHURA'S SISTER

Shura and Ari didn't have much time to move their family and wares from a Herat platform to the train that would hopefully usher the family safely to Kokand, their native country. Walking brusquely with their heads down, Ari narrowly avoided colliding with an unfamiliar man. Startled, he looked up and met the stranger's dark eyes behind his round spectacles. He opened his mouth to apologize for nearly bowling him over but paused when he realized that he looked like a fellow Jew.

Hasid was dressed as a businessman in a three-piece suit and tie. He wore a fur *tarbush* that distinguished him from the Afghan men who wore *perahan turbans* wrapped around their heads several times with the left-over fabric hanging to the side.

"*Bebachshid*[1]," the man said as he bowed his head and placed his hand on his chest before she could speak, backing up slowly to give the family more space. "I didn't see you coming."

---

1 *Bebachshid (Dari)*– I am sorry

"*Chizi nist*[2]," Ari replied, apologizing. "We're late for our train." Shura adjusted the small colorful, embroidered patchwork bag on her shoulder and angled herself to walk around him.

Shura had Mongolian features, somewhat typical for Bukharan Jews with a round face and slanted eyes, except that Shura had blue eyes—a striking contrast. Hasid could tell she was Bukhari, and he found her attractive.

"You're not going to Herat?" he asked. There was a shadow of disappointment in his eyes.

"*Neh*," Ari answered. "We confused the platforms."

"*Shu'mah az Bucharai*[3]?" He asked directly, with a piercing glance at Ari.

"*Ah'ree*[4]," he replied, nodding yes. Familiarity overwhelmed them, comforting them. From then on, they spoke in Bukharian, a dialect of the Tajik-Farsi language that incorporated elements of Hebrew, as they were delighted to find some common ground.

The man introduced himself as Hasid Shamash. "I'm traveling back home to Herat." Hasid was born and raised in Turkmenistan in pre-communist Russia. His family sought to escape persecution in the early 1800s in Mashhad and looked for better business opportunities and religious freedom. Already there was commonality—language, persecution, religion, and now they all found themselves at the meeting point that would change their destinies.

Hasid often traveled through Central Asia, trading textiles, diamonds, and other commodities, but for now, Herat was his home. The strength of the Jewish merchants, like Hasid, lay in having a network of connections throughout the Russian and British empires. Letters, messages, culture, goods, and trade were

---

2 *Chizi nist (Dari)*– it's nothing
3 *Shu'mah az Bucharai (Dari)*– Are you Bukharan?
4 Ah'ree *(Judeo farsi)*– yes

all woven into this network. Hasid had family members, each living in a different city along the route of the goods traded. One would buy merchandise and send it to a brother in another town, who would, in turn, purchase local merchandise and send it to the others, each living in a different town. The easiest and smallest items to trade and move were diamonds—put it in your pocket or sock, sew it into a garment, and go.

Standing in the hot sun and staring into the earnest face of a fellow Jew, Shura and Ari forgot how much of a hurry they were in. The family made conversation with Hasid, gaining the courage to eventually ask the question most on his mind: the woman was married, of course, but did Shura have any single sisters? Ari almost laughed at the directness of his question but instead smiled and gave his reply by lifting four fingers to his chest.

"Here? *Kiboud*?[5]" Hasid asked, gesturing behind him in the direction of Mazar.

"In Kokand," Shura cleared her throat and clarified, "That's where we're going."

Hasid's wide, earnest eyes brightened at her words. Since Hasid was a traveling merchant, he rarely had an opportunity to meet women, and he was a bachelor ready to get married. Standing before him was a couple who shared common ground with him. An instant camaraderie developed. Hasid pushed forward asking where to find Shura's family in Kokand in the hopes of making a marriage offer to one of her sisters. Dora, Shura's older sister who was twenty-five years old, was the most viable option, as the other sisters were much younger. A chance encounter had altered the trajectory of Hasid's life and maybe Shura's.

Traveling from Herat to Kokand would be no small commitment. It was quite common for a bachelor in his travels to find a

---

5 *Kiboud (Judeo farsi)*– where?

woman from another city. Hence, engagements were always short, and marriages followed rather quickly. The distance between Shura's home and Hasid's was 1,480 kilometers. The Afghan government limited rail travel to insulate the country's culture from British and Russian influence. The difficulty of the journey did not deter Hasid; he was driven by possibility and hope.

While Shura and Ari were headed toward Kokand, Hasid arrived home in Herat. There, Hasid invited his sister-in-law Rachel to travel to Kokand to secure his future bride. It was quite an undertaking for a woman he had never met, but marriage was the absolute glue that bound Jewish communities together. Matchmaking and marriage were family affairs for Jews in the Bukharan community, where the population was limited. Partnerships hinged on family approval, with most families preferring to pair their children with someone well-known by the local community. Most matches were within the family itself or a circle of close family friends. This tradition consolidated wealth within one family and preserved Jewish culture in predominantly Muslim countries. It was predetermined, destined in a way, but also delicate.

Hasid donned his best clothes for the visit. Before entering the house of his future bride, he wiped off his sweaty palm and lovingly touched the *mezuzah*[6] on the family's doorpost. Though nervous, Hasid conducted himself with calm dignity during the journey. He exchanged jokes and stories with his sister-in-law, Rachel, en route. She was the best person to join him in this venture because she had family in the Fergana region who could vouch for Hasid. Rachel spoke fluent Russian since she lived

6 *Mezuzah* - a piece of parchment inscribed with specific Hebrew verses from the Torah, affixed to the doorposts

in Soviet Turkmenistan. There was commonality, and she would serve as a bridge between the two families should the courtship progress. Bringing her was an act of faith designed to earn the trust of his bride-to-be and her family. They arrived in Kokand tired from the long trip.

Unfortunately, Hasid's arrival was ill-timed. The woman he was hoping to court had just suffered a death in her family. She had lost her grandmother, Zolicha. When he entered Shura's house, it was buzzing with people paying *shiva*[7] calls. Shura's mother, Bracha and other family members were sitting on the floor covered in Bukharan red wool carpets and wearing traditional white mourning garbs with black stripes. The women had their hair covered in silk kerchiefs as a sign of modesty during this mourning period.

In the dining area, a table covered in a red *suzani* patterned tablecloth was set with mourning foods: *non toki*, a flat bread resembling matzah that is round and domed, eggs, fried fish with garlic sauce, and a fried spiral pastry called *hushquiliq*.

How would this *shiva* period affect their luck and future? Instead of paying a jovial first visit, Hasid and his family made a *shiva* call. "May your Bibi's memory be a blessing," Hasid offered.

A heavy-set, red-haired woman with a kerchief on her head, wearing cotton *ikat* garb, walked into the family room. She stood in the center of the room, eyeing the mourners, bowing her head. She was a *sozanda*—a professional female entertainer who sang and danced to *Shashmaqam* music, a genre with spiritual sounds and words to connect the Divine to the mourners. She belted out a sad melodious song that brought the mourners to tears. As she opened her mouth, she displayed a band of gold teeth. She sounded as if she was crying, but the song helped the family purge their feelings of loss.

---

7 *Shiva*– a seven-day period of mourning at home following the burial of a loved one

When there was a lull, Hasid turned to Shura and asked, "*Ki'boud Dora?*"

"Ah," Shura replied, blushing, "*Khar' meh kouneh[8].*"

"Work?" Hasid asked, not masking the surprise in his voice. In a matter of seconds, he realized that if he went forward with the proposal, he would marry a modern woman. Kokand had far more to offer women than Afghanistan and significantly more than Hasid's rural Herat. The match was going to be challenging in terms of managing expectations.

The home was spacious and elegant, situated off the street and well away from the noise and dust of the city. The interior also reflected family wealth, with summer or winter rooms to suit the season's climate. An upright piano sat in one of the rooms to play and entertain the family.

They told Hasid that Dora was an avid piano player. Hasid was impressed. He and his family engaged Dora's family, the Yugadayevs, in a stilted conversation about Zolicha and the increasing oppression of Jews in Kokand and the general area. When Hasid fell into nervous silence, Rachel forged ahead, making conversation in Russian—the mother tongue of both families.

When Dora finally returned home from her job as a bookkeeper, Hasid was eager to meet her. He rose to greet her. Dora had been expecting Hasid's visit, but not necessarily on this particular day. Her deep blue eyes blinked in surprise when she saw Hasid's family gathered with her own; her delicate lips drew back in an astonished gasp.

"Dora," Hasid said, unwavering in his eye contact. With her snow-white skin and sable-colored, coiffed hair that framed her deep blue eyes, she was as beautiful as he had imagined. She stood

---

8 *Khar' meh kouneh (Judeo farsi)*– at work

tall and erect with perfect posture, confidence radiating from her. She also had a very distinctive and defined dimple on her chin.

"Thank you for coming to the shiva," she said, the hint of a smile playing over her features. Dora could see Hasid's kindness and humility in how he held himself, and she heard it in his voice's low, gravelly cadence. Hasid could tell from her clothing that she was a modern woman—educated and carrying herself with dignity despite all her family had endured.

"My daughter works to support the family," Bracha interjected. "After my husband..." She trailed off, wringing her hands and looking to Rachel for approval.

"Things are different here in Kokand," Shura offered in support of her family's choices.

Rachel nodded in compassion. She understood hardships. She, too, had to work to provide for her family. When her husband Haim traveled for work, there were times when he had no money to send back home or his merchandise was confiscated, and Rachel had to roll up her sleeves and make homemade cheese and wine to sell in the local *sarai*[9].

Dora openly shared with Hasid that their family fortune was in decline, and their money brought them unwanted attention from their non-Jewish neighbors. Her father was a merchant, making frequent trips to Moscow, and had drawn the attention of Stalin's intelligence taskforce, the Joint State Political Directorate—the OGPU, the secret service of the Soviet Union. The OGPU targeted Dora's father in their attempt to "purge society of religion." His status as a wealthy Jewish man, trading in gold and frequently traveling to Moscow, made him a prime target. He was apprehended on a trip from Moscow and sent to a Siberian prison.

---

9 *Sarai (farsi/dari)*– market

The OGPU offered Dora's family one chance to free him—the price was the entire family fortune. Family was everything, so the decision required no deliberation. Panicked, the family dug up all of the gold and silver hidden around the property for emergencies such as this. Most Jewish families knew better than to rely on banks—essentials were kept at home, often hidden, so that it was readily accessible in times of need. Persecution was more a matter of when than if. Their foresight proved essential.

Unfortunately, and predictably, the OGPU was not good on their word. They confiscated the family fortune, and Dora's father remained in a workers' camp in Siberia for three years until his body could no longer take the hard labor and frigid temperature and he died.

Hasid found himself sitting across from Dora's mother, Bracha, nervously slurping his *choi* from a tall glass and willing himself to find the right thing to say. Maybe, he thought, his bride-to-be wasn't modern but merely strong. Strong by necessity, given that she lived in a world that treated her family so cruelly for their religion and fortune. Hasid felt a surge of affection for Dora because his family story was similar to hers.

Hasid, in turn, shared a story of his father's deportation: "My parents held a large lavish *bar mitzvah* for my brother Haim in the courtyard of our home in Samarkand. Our home was palatial, and our family was known, and when the local people heard about this illegal Jewish ceremony, they reported us to the authorities. Immediately my father was extradited from the city and sent to live in Astarabad in Northeastern Iran."

Hasid paused. Dora listened intently. "They had no family or friends to ensure his safety, and he was at the mercy of the authorities there and likely to be killed. My family knew of an Iranian man living within their community and asked him to travel to Astarabad to check his safety and well-being. They sent this man with money to buy passports for my father and my uncles to become Iranian nationals rather than Soviet nationals to avoid religious persecution and economic sanctions."

Dora nodded at Hasid. She understood them. They shared a struggle, a history of persecution. By the end of the day, Hasid had proposed. Traveling merchants like Hasid had no time to spare for long courtships. They would be married within a month.

Hasid and Dora's betrothal ceremony, called *Shirin-khori,* took place in Kokand. It was called "Eating the Sweets'" and consisted of *sar-i quand,* or sugar lumps, whose sweetness, bright color, and multiple grains symbolized fertility, good luck, and success. A *jaroz,* or dowry, was traditionally given for the bride's hand in marriage. Hasid's included custom-made bridal clothes, including summer and winter clothes, bedding, and several pairs of leather women's shoes. Hasid's family paid the expenses of the wedding.

The wedding day itself, *Ruz-quiddush,* was set for a Wednesday during the first half of the month, which was believed to be an auspicious time for conception due to the waxing moon. After the wedding, Dora and Hasid stayed home for a whole week. Family and friends would come over in the evenings for the *Shevah Brachot*— seven blessings recited for seven nights. This was a kind of honeymoon, and both did not work during that week. Bracha stayed with them during the week of *Sheva Brachot,* except on the first two days. This was custom to help transition her daughter to becoming a wife. In the first three days of *Ruz-quiddush*, Dora was not allowed to go out alone, only escorted by her husband.

Dora was pregnant in what felt like no time, and the couple was eager to return to Herat so that Hasid could resume his business ventures, traveling, and trading.

CHAPTER 4

INTERNMENT IN RUSSIA

We have a problem." Hasid sighed late one evening. "It's going to take three months before you can leave Kokand for Herat." Dora was cleaning up from dinner, and Hasid had been flipping silently through their travel permits.

Faced with continuing waves of refugees, Afghanistan's resources were overwhelmed, and its policies had become draconian, particularly for non-Muslims. There was a harsh response from the Afghan government, which began to see new Soviet refugees as a menace to national security and stability. Consequently, domestic policies were quickly reshaped to minimize these perceived risks.

"Three months?" Dora asked, her heart sinking. She paused and balled the rag she was holding into her fist. "What will you do?"

"What can I do in Kokand?" Hasid asked with a sigh, pressing his hands to his eyes. "I have nothing to buy or sell. Nothing to sell means no living for us."

"I wish we had something left to sell," Dora whispered, closing her eyes and taking a breath. She ruminated over her luxurious lifestyle as a child. How did her circumstance in life change so drastically? Mother Russia used to be so beautiful.

"*Kai'muram kai'muram[1],*" whispered Dora under her breath shaking her head. If the OGPU hadn't stolen their family fortune. If only her father were still around. *If only.*

"I'm going to have to return by myself," Hasid said apologetically, "to Herat."

Dora responded with a nod of agreement, although she was devastated. Even though she'd known this could happen, how would she be able to live without Hasid for a few months? Still, she resolved to stay strong.

When Hasid left for Herat with promises of returning in a few months, Dora didn't cry as she watched him go. She held a glass of water in her hand and threw the water behind him, as was the custom for safe travel. According to folk belief, throwing water behind the person who goes on a journey symbolizes mobility and wishes that their journey will go as smoothly as spilled water runs.

She offered a dignified wave and heartfelt well-wishes, and prayed for his safe return while she watched his receding figure against the bright morning sky.

Three months later, Hasid did return safely, and he returned with diamonds. In Communist Russia, possessing diamonds was against the law, so trading in them was quite dangerous. Much like Dora's father, Hasid didn't trust the local banks. When he was not meeting with prospective clients, he stored the diamonds

---

1 *Kai'muram (Judeo farsi)*– when am I dying?

at home. Just like Bracha had worried about her husband, Dora worried about Hasid. Every day, she waited for his return and fervently hoped nothing would go wrong. One day, Hasid rushed through their front door with wild, worried eyes and Dora knew something was amiss.

"What happened?" Dora asked, rushing to Hasid's side.

"Someone—a *charidor*[2]—reported to the OGPU that I have diamonds," he hissed. Dora's heart sank. "I told them that yes, yes I do," Hasid replied evenly.

"Why did you tell the truth?" Dora asked. Her words were not accusatory, only surprised.

"*Neh meh doh'nam*[3]." Hasid shrugged. "The words tumbled out of my mouth so quickly, as if G-d himself put them there."

"And then what?" Dora urged him on.

"I lied and said that the diamonds weren't with me, but I promised that I would report with the diamonds in the morning."

"They will arrest you," Dora said, shaking her head.

"I will have to leave the country," Hasid sighed, the weight of the day's events pressing down upon him and leaving him scared and exhausted. The couple knew there was no time to grieve; they had to act soon. Together, they left for the market and used Hasid's numerous community connections to hire men to smuggle him across the border to Afghanistan. The smugglers would take him that very night. With another tough goodbye ahead of her, Dora focused on packing food and water for Hasid.

The road to Afghanistan would be hard—much harder than his other trips across the border. In the past Hasid had traveled with other tradesmen, who would sojourn in groups for protection, with many horses and caravans. This time he would be

---

2 *Charidor (Judeo farsi)* – a buyer or customer
3 *Neh meh doh'nam (Judeo farsi)*– I don't know

traveling alone. Hasid had to risk trekking through dangerous and mountainous terrain where Turkmen would attempt to loot merchants. The dusty roads along the jagged mountain peaks were prime hiding spots for thieves—This was a danger that they could not afford, so instead, Hasid and his smugglers walked. They walked doggedly through the nights, no matter the weather, trying to escape any attention, then hid and slept in caves in the mountains during the day. The distance between Kokand and the Afghani border would be nearly seven days on foot. But the arduous journey proved to be prudent. Not even a full day after Hasid departed, the OGPU paid their home a visit. Dora answered the door, dressed modestly and breathing evenly to calm herself.

"Where is your husband?" an officer demanded, speaking in Russian. The agents filled Dora's doorway with their olive-green uniforms, knee-high, muddy leather boots, and sharp red vizor caps bearing the Soviet star.

"*Ya ne znayu*[4]," she pretended not to know and shrugged her shoulders. "He often travels for business."

"Tell us where he is," the officer demanded again, "or we'll arrest you!"

"*Ya ne znayu*," Dora insisted. She lied again. She was scared now, but she was also out of options. One of the officers lunged at Dora, grabbing her by the wrist and pulling her from her home. She would serve an indeterminate jail sentence for an indeterminate crime.

Soviet prison was dark, dreary, and perpetually damp. As Dora's eyes adjusted to the darkened indoor atmosphere, her mood adjusted to match the depressing setting. Her daily work

---

4 *Ya ne znayu (Russian)*– I don't know

became a disheartening cycle of writing appeals for her freedom in Russian. Writing until her hand was cramped and her vision blurred, she made applications to the prison attendants, the greater Soviet officials, and anyone who could help obtain her release. All the while, her pregnancy advanced. When she had nothing else to do—which was often—she would place her hand on her growing belly and wait for the child to move. The growing baby gave her a reason to care for herself and keep her spirits alive.

Nothing with Dora's pregnancy seemed to suggest any medical complications, but even with a staff of nurses advocating for her health, giving birth to her first child in prison was risky. Maternal and infant mortality concerns loomed, and she was equally worried about the emotional toll that giving birth alone in prison would take. And she indeed had reason to be concerned as her sister Shura suffered miscarriages and stillbirths living in the rural city of Herat with no medical care available for women. She was fearful that she might suffer the same fate.

Although they had no control over her release, the nurses on staff remained a constant source of emotional and physical support. Each time they checked on the baby's growth or offered Dora a soft word of encouragement, she felt her strength double or triple in magnitude. Her pristine Russian education, too, was a boon, not only because it allowed her a greater understanding of the application process for her release but also endeared her to the nurses who respected her education and her tenacity. The nurses understood that they were all part of the same class of working, educated women, regardless of Dora's imprisonment.

But the months spun forward without any hope of her release. On an early morning at the end of 1933, Dora woke up to cramps that she had never felt before. The cramps grew stronger and stronger until she knew for certain that she was in labor. Under the harsh and dreary lights of the prison, Dora labored for hours, saying psalms, and envisioning a healthy, strong child at the end of the ordeal. Under the care of prison nurses, she gave birth to a daughter: Zolicah, named, of course, after her departed Bibi. It was custom amongst Bukharan Jews to name your children after their grandparents, living or departed.

Dora paused and thought that a Jewish-sounding name might cause problems for her little Zolicah, so she erred on the side of offering a Russian name. When the nurses asked for her name, Dora said something else. "*Etta*[5] *Zina*," she told them, staring dreamily into her daughter's eyes.

Zina spent the first six months of her life in prison. She was a delightful child—calm and content most of the time, but Dora worried endlessly that her child would die in infancy in jail. Against all odds, the child grew, and Dora continued to work for their release. When her release was finally secured, she didn't think twice about the fact that she would have to travel with Zina on horseback, as that was the only option to travel undetected to Herat. After all, they were non-citizens. Strapping the infant to her chest, Dora left for Afghanistan with another mother-child duo, carrying their meager belongings and their hopes for a better future for their children.

Dora understood that making it across the border would not guarantee her safety. She wouldn't feel safe until she made it to Herat, where her husband was anxiously waiting.

In Afghanistan, Hasid arranged with a well-known Afghan Jewish smuggler. He helped other Jews flee the Soviet Union by bribing the Afghan ambassador with 50 rubles per person, which obtained him an Afghan passport for Dora. This would ensure their safety once they arrived in Afghanistan as "nationals."

---

5 *Etta (Russian)*– this is

Always resourceful, Dora made contact with her husband using the same type of smugglers who had helped Hasid out of Kokand over a year ago. These men were professionals in their trade, smuggling information as often as they smuggled people. Rather than rely on mail, the smugglers took slow and safe routes by foot. They delivered messages in person, keeping contact open between Dora and Hasid while she worked her way toward the border. When they made it to the border, she was greeted with an automobile that Hasid sent to pick them up. She wept with relief.

Finally, she and Zina were free from prison and the constraints of Soviet rule. But, life in Herat, Afghanistan, was not the freedom Dora could have hoped for, neither for herself nor her infant child. Their challenges as a family were not ending but changing.

CHAPTER 5

IN THE HEART OF HERAT

Dora held Zina close in her arms. She wanted to comfort her as their ride rambled into the city of Herat. Once a multicultural place made famous during Alexander the Great's conquest in 330 B.C.E, Herat was famous for its imposing citadel and its vibrant economic life. It was perfectly situated along the Silk Road—north to Russian territories, east to China, south to Persia, and west to Constantinople.

As Hasid greeted her, Dora introduced Zina and gently spoke a Russian phrase that means meet your family.

Hasid placed his index finger to his mouth and whispered, "Dora, don't speak Russian here; they will think you are a spy. From now on, we speak Bukhari."

To align herself with the attendants in prison, Dora was accustomed to speaking Russian to Zina. Now, she would have to adjust her language and reorient as she re-entered society.

All Dora wanted to do was speak privately with Hasid. It soon became apparent that there were other priorities at hand. The ladies from the community were off to the side, and as soon as they saw Dora, they quickly surrounded the car and all started talking at once. Dora blinked in surprise and tried to focus on the cacophony of voices. "The laws . . ." one woman said, shaking her head, "are important to remember." Dora felt suddenly dizzy. She nodded her head while hugging her baby tighter.

"Put this on—" another woman chimed in, handing a scarf to Dora. In rural Herat, a woman had to be covered.

Under the press and pull of the women's hands, Dora's dark hair vanished under a headscarf, and her body disappeared beneath a *chador*—a full-body length of fabric draped over the woman's day clothes. She felt hot and anxious. The chador was more to her than just a cloth covering. It was the symbol of her suppression and a stark reminder that with every step forward, it felt like she was pulled backwards. Yes, she was free from prison bars, but now she was in a different prison- a much more elusive one. The high walls of the compound were meant to shut everyone in and shut everyone out. No one was meant to see what went on behind these walls, and no woman was supposed to see anything on the outside.

"Blue," someone spat out. Dora thought, at first, they were talking about her eyes. "For the market. The blue *chador*[1] is for *Yahudis*[2]. Never leave the *mahalla*[3] without putting on blue."

Dora knew she was different. She was very tall with Eurasian features. And stuck out as she'd not been covered up. "Blue," Dora

---

1 *Chador*- a large piece of fabric covering the upper body and head with only the face exposed.

2 *Yahudi (farsi)*- Jewish

3 *Mahalla (farsi)*- closed quarter

repeated in a daze. She adjusted her new headscarf and followed the women along the road to their home.

That night, Dora finally sat down with Hasid for a brief conversation. He was anxious about their arrival, given the ordeal Dora had to endure at the onset of their marriage. Their life together has started with so many challenges and time apart. Hasid did not know if Dora would react to her imprisonment for covering up his escape, nor did he know how she would respond to a country that was more backwards than Kokand. He eyed baby Zina reverently but nervously, as it felt he'd skipped from bachelor to fatherhood. This was all new to him. Dora let Zina sit on her knee, drooling and bouncing, while the couple caught up.

"I hope you will be *khoobeh*[4] here in Herat." Hasid looked with some apprehension at his wife, then with love and relief at the survival of Zina, a miracle child.

"*Neh meh doh'nam*[5]. There is a choice?" Dora replied, tired and overwhelmed. She sunk into her chair, aware she had a new life, yet again.

"Should I?" Hasid asked, gesturing to the baby.

Dora wasn't used to parting with Zina, and Hasid was unlikely to spend much time caring for the baby anyway. "Tomorrow, tomorrow," she insisted with a weak smile.

Division of labor in Herat was heavily gendered. Men like Hasid were merchants and traders, while women ran the domestic sphere. Their *mahalla*, a two-story housing complex, surrounded a courtyard where eight to ten families shared nearly everything: outdoor toilets, a communal well, and an outdoor

---

4 *khoobeh (Judeo farsi)*– good
5 *Neh meh doh'nam (Judeo farsi)*– I don't know

tandoor—a central cooking space made of clay pots heated with a live flame of wood or charcoal that was left to smolder to retain heat. The women's lives revolved around household chores performed communally in the courtyard: grinding flour, cooking, baking, and washing clothes, as well as spinning, sewing, embroidery, and knitting. They made clothing for themselves and their children, items for the men, and all the family linens, including cotton pillowcases, blankets, curtains, and assorted bags. Sewing was a social occasion, especially in the preparations for Rosh Hashanah and Passover, when all family members received a new outfit. Also three months before a wedding and when a woman was in the third month of her pregnancy. To survive, you had to band together and support each other.

After months in prison, Dora was both heartened and overwhelmed by the number of people filling her tasks daily. Her new life was a difficult trade-off, but like she had told Hasid, it was the only option.

Sometimes, when cleaning or soothing Zina, Dora's mind would reflect on Kokand, and her heart would soften. She missed her mother and siblings. She needed them close to her to be part of raising her daughter. Her father's fate rested heavily in the back of her mind as she cooked and cared for Zina. In Kokand, she could have worked outside the home and sent Zina to better schools. In Herat, the joys of family life could so easily become consumed under the litany of women's work behind the village walls.

Dora's new life was, in most ways, more strenuous than her tidy life as a bookkeeper in Kokand. She could no longer anticipate the daily end of her work shift in the evening, as there was always another task, and each task had to be completed by hand. The *tandoor* ovens had to be kept at a certain temperature, water had to be hauled from the well—for cooking, drinking, and bathing—and the outdoor kitchen was a walk away from their apartment. These household tasks had to be completed no matter the weather. The heavens sent Dora flooding rains, below-freezing temperatures in December, and 100-plus degree heat in the summer. She accepted the harsh daily realities of her world with steely resolve.

"They are sending Jews from all over the country to live here," Hasid told Dora one morning at breakfast, his voice soft and his expression inscrutable. He moved his eggs around his plate, fresh from the clucking hens. Hasid's business was facing new economic hardships as Jewish relationships with the Muslim population changed via government edicts.

"There was an edict just after the assassination of the Shah," Hasid explained, spitting out the word *edict* like it was cursed. Bukharan men had maintained economic relationships with Afghan Islamic governments for hundreds of years. Merchant Jews were considered neutral parties and were often the only ones allowed to venture into disputed tribal territory. Afghan Kings concerned themselves with maintaining dynastic lines and wrangling tribal affiliations under central control. They were more concerned about staving off British colonialism and Russian conquest than they were with a few thousand Jews. "All Jews have one month to return to the cities of their birth. For most Jews, that means here—Herat."

"But how many?" Dora wondered.

"*Ha'mesh Ha'mesh*," Hasid admitted. "A lot."

"But our neighbors . . ." Dora protested, worried that an influx of Jews would draw the ire of their Muslim neighbors. They knew quite well that the Muslim people of Herat fed into the fears of the Jewish *other*.

Hasid shook his head. It was becoming harder to live and more dangerous to make a living. The Jews had a brief revival under the rule of King Nadir Shah from 1929 to 1933, as he had successfully reversed many of the decades-old anti-Jewish decrees and gave Jews equal rights as citizens. But disaster struck when the king was assassinated by his son. Nazi propaganda filtered into the country, causing more pogroms and the ghettoization of Jews in Herat. Harsh economic laws drove many Jews to be restricted to the cities of Herat, Kabul, and Balkh.

"There is nothing we can do." Hasid sighed. The conversation was over. All they could do was hope that tensions wouldn't spiral out of control. And for a while, it looked like their hopes would come to fruition.

But then, that summer of 1935, just a few months after Dora and Zina arrived, Hasid informed Dora some alarming news. "It's a disaster! A Jewish boy and a Muslim boy in the city center got into a fight that grew uglier . . . and more physical. As the fight concluded, the Muslim boy fell down a flight of stairs, and the Jewish boy was arrested."

"*Ibi Ibi*[6]. What? Why? " Dora wasn't used to Hasid speaking with such urgency.

"Rumors had spread that the Jewish boy attempted to convert the Muslim boy to Judaism. Now there is a riot in Herat."

"A riot?!" Dora asked, her heart racing and palms sweating, cupping her abdomen. She was pregnant with their second child.

"They're raiding Jewish homes," Hasid shared, his voice laced with pain and anxiety. "Jews are also being beaten in the streets. Women are sexually assaulted." Dora collapsed her head into her

---

6 *Ibi ibi (Judeo farsi)*– a saying when there is something dreadful

hands in horror. Hasid didn't tell Dora the extent of the violence, though. He didn't want to worry her while the violence was mostly confined to the city center. Dora tasked herself with staying calm for the developing child's sake. Dora's pregnancy with Zina had been frightening enough not having the aid of her family, or support other than what the prison doctors and nurses could provide.

What he chose not to tell her was this: Mobs were rushing through the ghetto, shrieking: "You're filthy! Despicable! You deserve to die!" Rioters grabbed whatever they could in their hands and broke windows, crashed through gates, and broke into homes, terrorizing families. They pillaged whatever struck their fancy—household furnishings, gold, silver, rugs. They eyed little girls, raped them, and then called them "whores." It was merciless.

In the wake of the violence, Jews closed their businesses. Butcher stores and stalls at the *sarai*[7] sequestered themselves behind their walls, praying that the violence would diminish. Many families fled east to the capital city of Kabul—a full day away, even by automobile.

The family remained in Herat through the heat and lingering violence of the summer. But Dora was increasingly concerned. In Herat, there were no safe and proper facilities in town for women to give birth. And even if there had been a hospital that was a reasonable distance, there were no hospitals for women. Furthermore, there were no doctors behind the walls of the Jewish community. Becoming a doctor required education, so medicine was a profession beyond what was available to a Bukharan man.

Dora screamed, intoxicated with pain that felt like she was being ripped apart, directing faith and goodwill toward her

---

7 *Sarai (farsi)*– market

birthing child, until finally, a healthy baby girl emerged. The birth would be the most difficult of her eight birth experiences. It was without any pain medication or proper medical attention. A local midwife did her best to keep Dora comfortable, but rural Herat made any care difficult. "Even though your *dadeh*[8] cannot be by our side, you will know him soon." She wrapped her daughter in a blanket, soothing her and crooning to her, keeping a constant watch on the infant while she recovered from labor. As she held and rocked her baby, she prayed to G-d to give her family wings. *Please,* she pleaded, *give us wings to fly away from Afghanistan.* And then and there, Dora named her newborn, Zipora, meaning "bird."

---

8 *Dadeh (Judeo farsi)*– father

KABULI CLAN

"I am gaining my strength back," Dora told Hasid one evening after dinner. "I'm ready to leave here." Zipora was swaddled in her arms, and Zina held onto her leg.

"What we do not have," Hasid replied, "are permits, we would need permission." A forlorn expression fell on his face, and frustration ricocheted in his voice. "From both Britain and Afghanistan. We are considered Soviet refugees."

"And we can't get it?" Dora asked in a mix of disbelief and fear. She'd set down the children to play. She did not want them to worry.

Hasid shook his head. There was sadness in his eyes. "Afghanis are pushing the narrative that *Yahudis* are criminals and communists. British officials believe them and are holding back on granting permits for us to enter their colonies!" Hasid wished he could better protect his family. "Our only choice is to move east to Kabul."

"You're right." Her true desires were to be close to her mother and siblings back in Kokand, but her rational self knew that

Hasid could not make a living there, and it was also customary for a wife to live with her husband's family. Ultimately, she felt that Palestine was the safest and most viable place to live for a Jew. No more persecutions, no more running. Free to live, work and get educated as a Jew. Nonetheless, she responded, "Kabul's a more modern city. Better we go there for now, until we figure out our next move." She cursed under her breath in frustration. "*Jhoni margh[1], Afghanistan.*"

"The capital it is, then," Hasid agreed. "I think my business will be better there. I can move around more easily and export goods to other cities."

Once again, the Shamash family—with Zina almost three years old and Zipora still an infant—traveled in a *gaudi*[2] to Kabul where Hasid's brother Shimon and his wife Zipor, were already residing. They would join them in their complex. And they hoped and prayed for the best possible outcome.

"Give this to Ap[3] Zipor." Dora handed her sister-in-law, white mulberries that Zina had just picked, cleaned, and placed on a tray to hand from across their roof. White mulberry trees, known as *toot*, grow wild all over Afghanistan due to its excellent moist soil and mountainous terrain. The branches brush over the rooftops and, over time, drop *toot* all over the roofs, making the roofs quite sticky and smelly. And Zina loved to show her usefulness.

Since homes were built so close together, it was possible to pass food items from one flat rooftop to another without

---

1 *Jhoni margh (Judeo farsi)*– you should die
2 *Gaudi (Dari)*– horse and carriage
3 *Ap (Judeo farsi)*– aunt

descending into the street. Roofs were actively used in the summer months for socializing and sometimes sleeping, but now, for the holiday season, they were used for shared food preparations. Zipor nodded from across the roof, and Dora smiled, "I showed Zina when it's best to pick them off the tree, when they are long and white. When you dry them in the sun, they taste like honey."

"Shimon, see you soon for Rosh Hashanah," Dora called past Zipor, who lived in the adjoining household. Their home was made of sun-dried brick, connecting several families in a multi-family, u-shaped, two-storied complex.

Dora's one-bedroom apartment was insulated with carpets sprawled on the floors. On the walls, there were handmade Afghan-knotted wool carpets in rich jewel tones of red, blue, and gold featuring fine detailing in dark blue and black thread. Some carpets had "elephant's foot" patterns in rows and columns. Others had plant motifs woven in an angular geometric style featuring strong reds with dark edge detail. The rugs were a necessary accessory that created an inviting space, in contrast to the rest of their sparsely furnished apartment.

"*Rachmat*[4]," Shimon said with gratitude and shied away. Dora noted how different he was to Hasid, who was much more humorous and relaxed. Shimon was a well-tailored man—elegant, soft-spoken, very reserved, and respected amongst the upper class of Afghanistan, who knew him by his Muslim name, Shaban.

"Do you know when Hasid will return?" Dora asked.

"Hasid should arrive soon with the caravan." Hasid was on one of his many business trips where he traveled to remote caravanserais to conduct business and live in a solely male community for months out of the year.

---

4 *Rachmat (farsi)*– with pleasure

Caravanserais were needed as a place for safe shelter—not just from the extreme climates, but also from marauders who targeted caravans loaded with commodities. Caravanserais were separated one from the other at regular intervals so merchants would not have to spend the night vulnerable on the road. They were often built just outside the nearest town and resembled fortresses with high walls, a large gate that could be locked at night with heavy chains, and a guard at the entrance stationed for protection.

However, the interior did not mimic the exterior fortress. The ground-floor had a courtyard accommodating storage and stables for livestock and a corner for cooking in the tandoor ovens. On the second floor, there were sparse rooms for sleeping.

Hasid dealt in fabrics, dried fruits, karakul fleeces, second-hand clothing, yarns, and gold. As a byproduct of its safe respite, caravanserais also became a source for trading goods and culture for Hasid.

Dora wondered what Hasid would bring for them this time around. Whenever Hasid returned home, he would come with large quantities of staple foods that could be stored underground in their dried mud adobe silos.

Hasid was traveling back from Bombay, where his business partner, Pinchas Amram, had settled. Hasid would source merchandise in Afghanistan and bring it to Pinchas to sell. Pinchas and Zipor had previously been engaged. Pinchas was a traveling merchant and asked his good friend, Shimon, to look after his fiancé while he was away for business. Shimon's watchful eyes turned into a courtship as he lured Zipor away from Pinchas. There was some family strife over this, but living in India away from the couple, and finding another woman to marry, allowed Hasid to retain the partnership.

"Let's meet soon for *choi, kishmish*[5], and some *chach chach*[6] while we cook in the courtyard," Zipor suggested. "I will invite the other women." On the other side of the complex, in two apartments, lived the Khafi family and the Aharonoffs.

The courtyard had a well, and there the women would occasionally meet, sharing a little gossip, a few jokes, laughter and heartbreaking tears. Many of these women were raising children alone while their husbands were away on business. There was a sense of frustration at this secluded primitive life. They were each other's entertainment and therapy.

To add to the congestion, they kept a shed for sheep and raised chickens in a coop. Zina and her sister Zipora loved playing with the sheep. It was their pet. They had watched the sheep being sheared twice this year while their father sold the karakul wool to factories in Moscow. For cooking with oil, some of the wool was immersed in a pot of water to boil for hours, adding more water from the well in the courtyard, as needed, to counteract the evaporation. The wool was sieved through a cheesecloth to extract any impurities. When the grease cooled, it was stored in a cool shady place and used for meal preparation.

The women used the *tandoor* to bake *naan* with kosher flour. For this, the families in each housing complex pooled their funds and purchased their own wheat. They then spent hours sitting in the courtyard, cleaning the wheat, removing any pieces damaged by heat, riddled with holes from insects, or noticeably discolored or shriveled. Only the best could be sent to a kosher mill. Every week, bread was made for Shabbat, just enough to last for the weekend. Bread had to be eaten right out of the oven, otherwise if it was left to sit there, flies would infest it, and the sandy dust would blow into it.

---

5 *Kishmish (Judeo farsi)*- assortment of dried fruits
6 *Chach Chach (Judeo farsi)*- gossip or chit chat

"Zina, watch my hands mix the flour and water," Dora instructed as she churned it over and over until her fingers were sticky. "One day, you will be in charge of this, and you must consider the climate. On warmer days, the dough will rise faster, and the kneading is easier on the hands. On colder days, the yeast needs more rise time, and it can feel like a battle against the arms, but just let the dough rest for five minutes and then return to it and it will yield to you."

Dora's fingers were thick like sausages and full of warmth; perfect for rolling out the dough with the palms of her strong hands. She stuck the dough to the interior sides of the *tandoor* to bake and then peel it off from the oven walls when it was baked. The dough filled the air with a malty aroma as it transformed into golden, bubbling *naan*, bursting with flavor and crispness.

Nearby were storage rooms for food and firewood and an outhouse for toileting. Families shared the outhouse, which amounted to huge, deep holes dug into the ground. Adults took turns standing one foot on either side of an open pit, and the children were held high, because their legs were not long enough to spread and stand. The unsanitary situation led everyone to have issues with worms. It was very common to excrete worms due to poor conditions and lack of access to health facilities. Sometimes they would take an herbal elixir that would cause them to excrete dead worms. Dora would need to send Hasid to the local *sarai* to buy an elixir if he did not return home with one.

Looking out from the rooftop, through the camel-colored dusk of rural Kabul, Dora spotted a caravan approaching the *maharal*. She could see the *bash*, the caravan's leader. He had learned every path in the land and the dialects of the cities in his region. He cultivated expertise in shipping any type of cargo.

Goods were packed onto the animals with rope and covered in blankets and carpet. The *bash* was riding on the first camel, while the last camel in the line had a bell tied to it. In that way, if the *bash* dozed off and there was a sudden silence, he was alerted that someone may be trying to steal the camel at the end of the line.

Close business connections and trust between the Turkmen and Jewish communities along the Silk Road helped to strengthen the economy from Northeastern Persia to Central Asia and Afghanistan and provided mutual protection for both groups. Officially, businesses such as imports and exports were restricted to Muslims, so Muslim partners served as front men. The business was conducted largely in Persian but written in Hebrew script, shared between a worldwide network of agents. Hasid was linked through family scattered all over Central Asia. He spoke many languages that facilitated business transactions, Dari and Pashtu, Turkmen, some English, Russian, and Hebrew when necessary.

"Dahdeh!"

Zina screamed from the roof when she saw her father. Dora and her daughters rushed to embrace Hasid. The caravan arrived at the town gate just as Rosh Hashanah was nearing and Hasid was reunited with his family. The next day was filled with joy and preparations.

All the women in the complex lit the holiday candles to welcome in Rosh Hashanah. Then night came. The barely lit streets fell silent; so quiet that you could hear a dog bark on the other side of the mountain ridge that split the city. The night sky was obsidian— an opaque black, dusted with a multitude of stars.

The evening felt special and the Shamash's were elated to be together again.

A warm glow lit the room. Dora and her sister-in-law along with all their children sat opposite the men. Rosh Hashanah was strictly adhered to; if anyone from the community broke from the holiday or Shabbat, intentionally or unintentionally, the whole community fasted for twenty-four hours as a sign of repentance. This is how the Jewish community survived for thousands of years in Central Asia, by strictly adhering to Jewish law that kept the community tight in mutual responsibility.

Hasid and Shimon reclined against cushions placed on thick blankets, preparing for the blessings with the children for the Rosh Hashanah meal, which had a specific order in which blessings were recited over *simanim,* or symbolic foods. There were a plethora of symbolic foods displayed on the carpet with a long, *sofre* tablecloth: apples, honey, dates, beans, leeks, beets, squash, and pomegranate, with a sheep head at the center of the table. All these *simanim* were symbols to embrace good fortunes for the year ahead.

With each food item, the men, women, and children alternated turns reciting the blessings over the *simanim,* beginning with the dates. The Hebrew word for dates, *tamar,* resembles the word "end," or *yitamu,* representing the desire for the enemies to end their hateful conquests. Beans in Aramaic are *rubia,* which is similar to the Hebrew word for increase, *yirbu,* as in increase one's merits.

Then Zina picked up the plate of leeks, which are called *karti* in Aramaic which is similar to the Hebrew *karet,* a term for "cutting off." Dora and Hasid beamed with pride as little Zina proceeded: "Leeks represent our hopes that our enemies will be 'cut off.'" With the help of her father reading along, Zina recited the prayer.

The next food was beets, which in Hebrew sound like *silek* or "depart." Zina continued, "....that our enemies, haters, and those who wish evil upon us shall depart."

Zina held up squash, which in Aramaic is *k'ra*, and is reminiscent of the Hebrew word *kriah,* or "tear." "..... that the evil of our verdicts is ripped up and that our merits be announced before you."

Then Shimon picked up the bowl of pomegranates, their many seeds representing the 613 *mitzvot,* or good deeds. He said, "The seeds can also symbolize the many blessings we hope will manifest in the coming year."

The apples were passed around to dip into honey, representing hope for a sweet new year.

At the center of the table was the head of a recently slaughtered sheep. The same sheep the children had played with before the holiday. Rosh Hashanah translates as "head of the year," which is reflected by putting the sheep's head on the table. "May it be Your will, G-d and the G-d of our ancestors, that we are like a head and not a tail." While eating the head was a *mitzvah,* the children decided against it, sticking their tongues out in protest.

After the ceremonial meal, Dora and Zipor set out the Rosh Hashanah meal– a parade of platters. The women served the men first, as was the custom in this patriarchal society. They feasted, happy in their family. "Delicious dessert!" Zina exclaimed as trays of hybrid melons, luscious grapes, *kulcha*[7], *kishmish*[8], and nuts alongside fragrant *choi* permeating cardamom capped off the evening. There was an art to drinking *choi,* cupping it from the bottom or holding it at the top with your thumb and middle finger as you drew in a deep gulp with rock sugar between your teeth.

---

7 *Kulcha (Judeo farsi)–* a sweet bread pastry
8 *Kishmish (Judeo farsi)–* mixed dried fruit

On holidays and Shabbat, *Bet Knesset*[9] attendance was a given. The interconnected courtyards allowed men secret access into one another's home for prayers. Fathers and sons scurried like mice to the *minyan*, no matter the burning summer heat, dusty streets, snowy winters, or the downpours of the rainy season. All Jewish men prayed communally three times daily as religiously proscribed and socially enforced.

If by chance, someone didn't come, he received a visit to find out why he was missing. But there wasn't a physical sanctuary to attend. Only a *cheder*, a room within the home of a Jewish family that was set aside for communal prayer. These rooms were built specifically for that purpose, with high ceilings and a niche in the wall facing Jerusalem, where Torah scrolls were placed. Community members just as often led prayers as the *Rav*[10]. This *cheder* was also the only place Jewish education took place. After services, the men would form groups to study the Torah, Rashi, Talmud, and Kabbalah.

This close community would soon be even more full.

---

9 *Bet Knesset (Hebrew)*– House of Jewish Worship
10 *Rav (Hebrew)*– Rabbi

CHAPTER 7

MEDICALLY LACKING

"Shame on you! You had a girl," the men were murmuring, shaking their heads. Yafa, a third daughter, arrived on the 27th of Tevet 1938. Zina's big brown eyes widened, scared from what she was hearing as she entered the synagogue for her baby sister's naming ceremony. Zina clung to Dora like they were all one unit. She pulled on her mother to get closer, being careful not to tug on the baby and its swaddling. Each child was loved deeply by Dora and Hasid. And they were soothed when close friends and family arrived at the synagogue to throw sweets so that Yafa should be "blessed with a sweet life!"

Jewish women of the *mahalla* convened at Dora's apartment on a brisk afternoon with the food they'd cooked for the family as Dora recuperated from the delivery. They examined the infant and pointed out to Dora a strange indent on the soft part of her skull. The women shook their heads and offered Dora their condolences. "The baby will not live," they whispered, gesturing to Yafa's head. "*Dora*, leave her on the roof. If she survives, it will be a miracle.

If she dies, it is an inevitability that no one could have prevented. Her fate would be in *Elokim's*[1] hands." The women said their piece and left.

Dora clung more desperately to her daughter. She refused to act on the women's words and did not heed their primitive superstitions to leave her daughter outside to die. While Hasid was at work trying to provide for the family, Dora took matters into her own hands. She took her lips to the soft fuzz of Yafa's head and slowly sucked the indent away. She had no idea what she was doing or if it would help. Faith and her hope were on her side.

Yafa survived.

The very next year, after a slew of girls, Hasid and Dora welcomed a boy. They named him Moshe, after Dora's beloved father. Moshe's birth, was the happiest moment of the Shamash's lives, and was greeted with relief. A son was a hedge against economic uncertainty, for only men could provide for the family in this patriarchal society. But more were to come. Moshe was followed by three more beautiful sisters: Rosa, 13th of Av[2] 1940, Tamar, 6th of Iyar[3] 1945, and Hanna, 28th of Tishrei[4] 1946.

With each birth, Dora wrote in Russian each child's birthdate from a torn off sheet of the Afghan government regulated newspaper, *Islah*. She'd acquired the anti-foreign paper when the family's male servant had purchased a melon wrapped in the newspaper.

---

1 *Elokim (Hebrew)*– G-d

2 *Av (Hebrew)*– 11th month of the Jewish calendar that usually falls July/August

3 *Iyar (Hebrew)*– 8th month of the Jewish calendar that usually falls April/May

4 *Tishrei (Hebrew)*– 1st month of the Jewish calendar that usually falls September/October

Women were not allowed to leave the compound, and certainly not do their own food shopping.

At the time, a woman like Dora might give birth twelve or thirteen times, with only half the amount surviving into adulthood. Sometimes women didn't survive the births. Dora's dear sister, Shura, for example, died in childbirth after her thirteenth delivery of a stillborn. Five children prior survived, but ultimately the poor medical conditions in the British Indian Empire took a deathly toll.

Dora thanked G-d that she had healthy child after healthy child. Rearing and changing diapers were done as efficiently as possible with so many children and "nappies" to change. For bedtime, the toddlers' torsos were tied with a rope around the bassinet with a hole at the bottom to catch any excrement during the night.

As Dora kept birthing and mothering, the house and family were maintained with order and cleanliness as much as possible. Despite the tight quarters, the family managed to make the most of their space by using every inch of their home to the fullest. Dora and Hasid slept in the only bedroom, while Zina, Zipora, Yafa, Moshe, Rosa and Tamar slept in the dining area that doubled as a second bedroom, with makeshift beds, a few chairs, and a small table.

In the corner, a small metal wood burning fireplace provided warmth. Moshe's job was to gather wood to feed the fireplace every night. After a long day of housework and school, the family often gathered around the hearth, each taking a seat and sharing stories of their day.

At night, the siblings drifted off to sleep in the dining room, listening to their parents' voices as they talked late into the night. The children slept soundly, despite the tight sleeping arrangements and cold temperature, reassured by the presence of their parents.

However, the unsanitary conditions in Afghanistan made everyone vulnerable to disease. Afghans couldn't access high quality care; it barely existed. Most people went to the local bazaars, which supplied both traditional healers and pharmacies, bringing "cures" home. *Atars* were sidewalk vendors who sold herbs for treatment, while some even went to the local barber to perform "bloodletting." Medical attention was extremely limited.

By the time the other siblings were born and grown from infanthood, Dora and Zina had been through a lot together—from prison to long moves to Zina's first major illness. At six years old, Zina woke up from a deep sleep gasping for breath. "*Onah,*[5] I can't breathe!" Zina yelped.

Dora rushed to her side and felt her head burning up. "Open your mouth and stick out your tongue." Her glands were swollen.

The local remedies did nothing against the bacteria that was coating and obstructing her air passages. She continued to lose strength, and the glands in her throat swelled up further, making it even harder for her to breathe.

In desperation, Dora called in a German-Jewish doctor the family knew. There was a shortage of Afghan medical doctors, as there was a lack of medical schools for training. Under Muhammad Nadir Shah's rule, all British and Soviet nationals were forbidden from working in Afghanistan because their potential for political influence was feared. Consequently, German expertise was in high demand, as German nationals were willing to work in difficult conditions for a fraction of the wage that other Europeans demanded.

---

5 *Onah (Judeo farsi)–* Mother

Germany had ulterior motives for allowing Germans to live in Afghanistan. Afghanistan was concerned about Britain and the Soviet Union fighting against Germany. Her position as a buffer between these two large powers was threatened, which provoked great anxiety. By July 1939, Afghanistan was genuinely afraid of being invaded by the Soviet Union. Afghanistan accepted economic and military assistance from the Soviet Union with the caveat that it didn't turn into invasion. Afghanistan also asked for military guarantees from Britain, though it did not receive a sufficient response. This led Afghanistan to seek support from Germany, whose anti-Communist vitriol may have appeared comforting to Afghan leaders, who did not want to be caught between their two powerful neighbors. Afghanistan took advantage of Germany's interest in its key geographic position to make economic and political gains. Germany viewed Afghanistan as a crucial potential gateway to India, while Afghanistan looked for a third power to balance the competing rivalries of Russia against those of Great Britain. (Koplik, 2015)

"She has contracted diphtheria and we must isolate her," the doctor explained to a worried Dora, pacing back and forth anxiously.

"There is no space to isolate her. We live in a one-bedroom home.

The doctor looked defeated as he dropped his head. "I'm sorry, I don't think she'll survive without medical intervention."

Dora spurted out in broken English with a thick Russian accent, "But noh chospital for voman!" Dora was normally calm, but now she was panicking.

In a lightbulb moment, the Doctor said, "She will go to the men's hospital There is no time to consider other options. We must disguise her."

Dora hurriedly fetched her scissors and grabbed lops of Zina's hair chopping off her curly locks. Her hair came rushing down to the ground feverishly in par with Zina's high temperature.

"Zipora, ask *Appi*[6] for her son's pants and shirt." Quickly Dora dressed Zina in her cousin Sam's clothing and the doctor rushed her through the hospital doors as if she were a young boy.

Once inside an operating room, he removed the bacteria coating her throat and opened her airways with a cut. Zina lived, but she kept the small scar the doctor had made on her throat.

Zina was too sick to remember the operation, but she never forgot the recovery. Zina's family sent a young Jewish man with food every day, as there was no food served in the hospital. He also brought with him clean towels, fresh bedding, and even the prescribed pharmaceuticals, since all of this was lacking. Day after day he sat in her room and watched over her. He ensured no one found out she was female. The man played games with Zina during the day, showing her ball tricks, playing cards and making her laugh, assuring her that everything would be alright.

"Soon," he said, "You will go home to your family, strong and healthy." And she did return, bold and willful as ever.

"Help, *Onah*[7]!" Zina snorted. Zina was helping Dora sift chickpeas and was bored, and so had lodged a chickpea up her nose. Her mother looked over. "I was just blowing it out as a game." Zina shrugged.

"Here, sniff this!" Dora held out the black pepper so that Zina could sneeze it out. She never knew what would happen next, but she did know that due to the demanding workload of running the

---

6 *Appi (Judeo farsi)*– auntie
7 *Onah (Judeo farsi)*– mother

home, women were not always able to keep as close of an eye on their children as they wanted. Too many children and not enough parental eyes to watch as they stirred the pot, sheared the sheep, or picked through hills of uncooked rice grains.

When the children were healthy and feeling well, they jumped rope, played hopscotch or played with the sheep and chickens in the courtyard.

Yafa decided to make a kite out of old newspaper, twigs and twine. After much imagination and hard work, she assembled the kite and called her friend, Rivkah, to fly the kite with her in the courtyard. She was so proud that she had made the kite all by herself.

Yafa threw the kite into the sky, as Rivkah's eyes widened by how it flew, high and beautiful. They were both so excited, that they forgot about everything else around them. But then, a gust of wind came and the kite flew too high, slipped away, and got trapped in the large well nearby. It was hard to distinguish the well from the surrounding sand and rocks around the perimeter.

Yafa who was overwhelmed with the devastation of losing the kite ran after it, and not seeing the well in front of her, fell right in. Head first. She cried in a panic. *"Komak![8]"*

"Yafa, don't worry. I'm going to get help," Rivkah called, matching the panicked voiced of her friend.

A neighbor with a ladder came rushing to rescue Yafa from the well. The kite could not be saved, but Yafa was spared, yet again.

"Come quick!" Zina yelled one day when she was twelve years old. Dora rushed out of the kitchen. "Moshe was

---

8 *Komak (farsi)*– help

carrying a pair of scissors around the house, and I just tried to take the scissors so he wouldn't hurt himself." Zina explained, starting to sob as Dora came rushing in.

Moshe who was just seven years old had blood seeping out of his eye. He had twisted away from Zina and tripped on the blade of the scissors, which went straight into the corner of his eye.

"Moshe will need to go to a hospital for an operation," Dora said firmly, trying not to lose her composure. Hasid was away on a business trip, and Dora had to do something quickly. *I'm not allowed into a hospital, let me get help from the neighbors*, she thought. Fortunately, the neighbor offered to take Moshe on their horse to the hospital in the city center. Moshe's vision was saved, but he was cross-eyed for years after the incident.

But at least Moshe had the option of hospital care, Dora thought with a bitterness that kept staining her exhausted heart.

"*Khanom!*[9] Rosa is injured." The maid who lived with the Shamash family came rushing into the kitchen, with Rosa bleeding and sobbing. Once again, Dora was distracted by her domestic duties. This time, Dora was preparing for *Sukkot* the next day, a fall harvest holiday. Rosa was inconsolable.

"I did not hear her." Rosa was the one constantly getting scraped up and requiring what little medical attention Dora or the local doctors could provide. A tiny tomboy, Rosa was fond of her games of climbing trees, hanging on the branches, and climbing up to the rooftop of their apartment complex. Rather than chiding her creativity, she held her and cleaned her up.

"What would we do without you?" Dora said to the maid. "You rescued her!"

---

9 *Khanom (farsi)*– madam

"*Rachmat.* I heard Rosa's cries from my quarters. I found her dangling from the roof, held up by a nail into her flesh. She cried and screamed and tried to wriggle free, but the nail kept tearing further through her skin. I had to climb a ladder to unhook her arm from the twisted nail."

Rosa was scared and numb and could not stop crying. The maid put her arm around Rosa and try to comfort her by patting her back.

Dora hurried with a sheet to twist around Rosa's arm to stop the bleeding. "She must've tried to catch herself, flinging out an arm." Dora was trying to process how dangerous it was.

The sheet quickly became saturated with blood. "The bleeding is not stopping. The wound is too large. Rosa needs a hospital." With a sigh of frustration at the lack of medical care, Dora said ". . . I will take Rosa to a local doctor instead."

The local doctor held Rosa still and, with needle and thread, stitched up Rosa's arm as best he could, given the extent of the injury. Rosa would have a large scar down her arm for the rest of her life, but she survived.

AN EDUCATION

"Walk out. You will walk out." Dora insisted. *School had become a reality for all her children, even the girls and it took some burden from her and maybe guaranteed a brighter future.* But she was tired of them hiding their Jewish identity. "When the teacher brings out the Quran, walk out of the room."

Dora's demand weighed on her mind. *We have hidden their Jewish identity as best as we could. Am I risking their anonymity? They might be bullied or beaten up.* Dora finished scrubbing her children's school clothes against the washboard. *Jewish children are not legally barred from enrolling.* Afghan schools, however, had an Islamic component, where each day set aside time to read the Quran; the family knew too well when Moshe would often brag to his sisters that he shared a class with the Afghan crown prince, Ahmad Shah Khan. No one, teacher or students, knew Moshe was Jewish, under his Muslim alias name, Mussa.

Their teachers, of course, would not take kindly to this. Moshe and the handful of other Jewish boys were removed from the classroom entirely when the teacher discovered that there were Jews learning alongside the crown prince. And when it was discovered that Yafa was Jewish, the teacher began taking a thin whip-like stick to the backs of her hands for alleged disobedience.

With little incentive to go to school, and a growing fear of punishment and mistreatment, the answer was simple: *don't go.* When Rosa became school-aged, Dora and Hasid stopped sending their children to Kabuli schools entirely.

Despite Dora's level of higher education, she decided that she would not force formal education on her children. There were no truancy laws to worry about, and it was considered easier to educate children in Torah through private tutors, ensuring that Jewish youth would not intermingle with their Muslim counterparts. Dora started to believe that Jewish isolation and insular schooling were the only way to protect their lives.

There was a farmer who had his milk stolen repeatedly. The farmer decides to stay up one night to see who was stealing the milk. He finds a monkey stealing the milk. So he takes a knife and cuts off the monkey's tail. The monkey yells, "I need my tail back!"

"I'll give you back your tail if you bring me milk," says the farmer.

"Okay, okay, I'll get you milk." The monkey takes a bucket to milk the cow. He explains to the cow that his tail has been cut off and he needs milk for the farmer to get his tail back.

"I would give you milk, but I don't have any milk to give. Feed me grass so I can make the milk."

The monkey walks a long time to find a field of grass, but all there is is dirt.

"Earth, I need grass to feed the cow to get milk to give to the farmer to get my tail back."

The earth says, "I can't make grass right now, I need water to grow the grass."

The monkey finds a well, but the well is dry. The monkey pleads with the well, "Please give me water to grow grass to feed the cow and get milk to give to the farmer, who will then give me my tail back."

The well says, "I need you to bring me some rain so I can fill myself with water."

The monkey looks up to the sky and asks for rain. "Sky, send rain to fill the well with water so that grass can grow in the field to feed the cow and get milk for the farmer, who will only then give me my tail back."

It rains. The well fills up with water. The monkey waters the ground for grass, the grass grows, and the monkey feeds the cow grass, which then makes milk. The monkey fills the bucket with milk and brings it to the farmer. The farmer says, "Okay, I'll put your tail back." He takes a needle and thread and stitches the tail to the monkey's backside.

The monkey is so happy he has his tail back. He strokes it and wags it around. He's so happy, but then the monkey has to make kha kha, but he realizes that the farmer has attached his tail over his backside. Now the monkey can't make.

Zina, Zipora, Yafa, Moshe, and Rosa were amused by this parable and listened intently to their new tutor sharing this story with such animation. Zina pushed on, "What is the point of this story?"

"To make you laugh. I heard this story when I was a child and it made me laugh too. My teacher shared it with me in class when she wanted our attention and this worked."

The children giggled. The story became engraved in their minds. It would be a parable that would one day be shared with their own families– their own version of story time.

With their attention, the tutor pushed on, "Between learning math and Torah, we're also going to learn sewing and embroidery." They quickly learned. And over the years, Zina and her sisters would share stories while cooking and sewing—a knowledge and a sisterhood.

Dora knew the children were fortunate to have a tutor, as not every family in the complex could afford their services. The Shamash's wanted their children to be educated . . . but educated the right way. *Though I have conformed in some ways to the thinking of the community, in other ways, I will not conform. I do not want our children married off at such a young age.* It was not uncommon for girls to be married off by fifteen years old.

Dora entered a cloud of thought. Hasid's older sister, Miriam, was twelve years old when his father was approached by a man *twenty years her senior* for her hand in marriage. *The father accepted his proposal, even though he was already married to another woman with whom he had children in another city.* Dora ruminated over how Miriam immediately conceived, and within a few weeks, this man absconded. Shortly after that, Afghans were expelled from Marv, and because Miriam was married to an Afghan Jew, she was considered Afghan by marriage. She was expelled from Marv, and the entire family moved to Samarkand with her. *All the traumas led her to give birth to a stillborn.* Dora sighed but stood firm. She would see to it that her children would receive as much education and time to be children as she could provide.

CHAPTER 9

AMERICA—THE DREAM BEGINS

Zina's first cousin Mayer, Hasid's nephew and the son of Haim, worked at the American consulate in Kabul, where he exchanged dollars for *afghani*—the Afghan currency. Jews were considered vital to the successful flow of trade because they were not subject to Islamic injunctions against usury and, therefore, could lend and exchange currency. Mayer had begun learning English as part of his job and teaching his relatives.

Through his work and connections, he became friends with an American Jewish couple, Ethel and Lenny Abrams, who were sent to Afghanistan by an American aid organization. Lenny was a civil engineer and contributed to Kabul's urban road development, just like he did in New York, being one of the engineers for the major highway, I-495.

In true Bukharan hospitality, Mayer invited them to his uncles Hasid and Shimon's home, for Shabbat dinner, knowing that they were looking to meet more Jews outside of their Bukharan circle and had a great desire to learn English.

"Tell me more about America," Zina piped up to her new mentors, Ethel and Lenny Abrams.

"Well, all boys and girls go to school together and can dress as they please. We all have access to medical care and all roads are paved and have cars and buses."

Zina's eyes widened, taking in all this information. Ethel could tell that Zina was hungry for an education.

"We are so lucky to have met you," Zina said with such excitement.

From that time on, the couple became staples in the lives of the Shamash family. Ethel wanted to travel throughout Afghanistan, but lacked the language to freely move around. Due to their kinship, Zina became Ethel's translator and partner in escapades as they traversed through Afghanistan.

Zina loved her parents, and she knew they adored her, but Ethel and Lenny shared a special bond with Zina, perhaps because they had no children. Zina felt them to be something akin to surrogate parents. They treated Zina with affection and always greeted her with a big hug. She was unfamiliar with that kind of physical warmth from her parents.

Adventurous and cosmopolitan, they dazzled the children with their vast knowledge and stories of exciting travel. They had, for example, had a home on the Ivory Coast. As the families grew closer, Ethel and Lenny told stories of America, a country that Zina had not even known existed, where Jews and non-Jews worked and lived together peacefully. Zina was fascinated and would repeatedly ask her new friends, "Share with us stories about America!" She was developing a newfound goal: the freedom to live as a Jew the way she wanted to live.

This everlasting affection would impact the whole Shamash family forever.

CHAPTER 10

ZINA IN PESHAWAR

"I see you," Dora whispered to Zina one night in bed. *Though you are only twelve, we are so alike,* Dora thought. Dora prayed for the family to leave Afghanistan, perhaps go to Palestine, to join her uncle Manny, and she sensed Zina's heart join her in prayer. Their longings stirred in their souls and shined from their eyes as they dreamed of what could become of their lives. Two women with an unwavering vision.

In bed at night, Zina dreamed of a bigger life, dreamed of a life outside of Afghanistan.

As the eldest of seven children, Zina was old enough to care for her siblings but still too young to have the type of responsibility and agency she craved. She enjoyed learning, but she hungered for more formal education than tutoring could provide.

Zina's doubts sometimes eclipsed her hopes. She saw how womanhood and marriage operated in Kabul, and the picture frightened her. She had seen how Afghanistan had worn on her mother, making her bitter. In a culture that kept girls close—fearing for their safety, their marriage prospects, and their insulated education—there was no possibility Zina could live outside of Kabul alone. *Where can I go?* she wondered. *And how can I bring my family with me?* Zina knew that her mother would never let her leave by herself; it was too unsafe. While Zina dreamed fervently of life with greater freedom, she didn't want to leave her family behind. The Shamash's knew they were better together than separated, no matter what challenges they confronted.

One morning, after a restless night of sleep, Zina woke up to the sound of her aunt, Ap Zipor talking to her mother. Zina overheard bits and pieces of their conversation: "To Peshawar . . . Hasid's family . . . Rachel . . . the Indian border."

"*Raft ah[1]* Peshawar?!" Zina blurted out. The two older women blinked in surprise at her sudden presence.

"Zina," said Zipor by way of greeting. "*Ah'ree,*" She nodded her head. "I am going to Peshawar to be with my family." Peshawar was a province in western British India that bordered Afghanistan.

Zina calculated her response: she knew her uncles and *Ap Shura* were there with cousins she was anxious to meet. She also knew it was a more modern city than Kabul.

"Please," Zina begged, turning her attention to her mother, her eyes wide and pleading. "I want to go, too. Can you please send me with *Appi*?"

"I have to ask *dadeh,*" Dora said finally.

---

1 *Raft ah (farsi)*- Are you going?

Dora hadn't seen her sister Shura since she married Hasid. Shura and Ari had moved to Peshawar. Dora longed for her family whom she hadn't seen since she left Soviet Uzbek so long ago. She did not want to deny Zina what she was deprived of– family.

Later that night, Dora talked to Hasid about the idea and he agreed. "Peshawar is on the border between India and Afghanistan. It's not too far from us and is under British influence and European modernity."

Hasid didn't want to discuss the overall politics with Dora but he continued to weigh the risks. World War II has only recently come to a close, and peace—especially within the borders of Europe's remaining colonies—was not guaranteed. "Zina will stay with my sister-in-law, Rachel," Hasid said.

Dora nodded in agreement. " . . . Shura is there, and her children are in school. Zina could get a good British education."

"I'll make travel arrangements," Hasid promised.

Zina was elated. There were no rail lines between Afghanistan and India, so she would have an automobile adventure. On the day of their departure, Zina carried her sack of clothing, almost as big as her body, out of their housing complex and into the waiting vehicle that would take her out of Afghanistan. It was the first time she would travel outside of the country since she had arrived as a baby. Fearless, she got into the car with Ap Zipor and left without shedding a tear. *I do not know when I will see the mahalla again. If I ever return, it would only be to collect my family and leave Kabul.*

The car drove over the bumpy road towards the Khyber Pass, a major trade route from East Asia to Europe. It was harrowing, with a sheer mountain on one side and a steep drop-off on the other. They drove through miles and miles of desolate desert which stretched out, hazy with dust and softly colored in an ombré of grays to purples. The twilight was long and had a hazy quality that seemed unchanging until suddenly, the night closed in and swallowed up the day. All the while, Zina's mind played back flashes of life in the *mahalla*: playing with sheep, handling wool grease, watching her siblings, daydreaming during tutoring sessions, and her mother's steady hands sorting rice grains. Her memories lulled her into a deep sleep, and by the time Zina woke up, she was finally out of Afghanistan.

Upon entering Peshawar, she noticed all the government and civic buildings were topped with minarets. "*Ohhhh, cheli cha'shan'geh!*[2] A city! Finally," Zina gawked. The driver explained that the buildings were structured around Islamic-style arches but were built using the British architecture techniques of the 1800s—concrete and steel. "Peshawar has been a revered, ancient city forever. It was once called the City of Men. Now it is called the City of the Frontier."

Zina had never lived in a city, and Peshawar, compared to rural Afghanistan, was astonishing.

The world outside her village felt bigger, more open, and connected than Zina had expected. In the city, Zina was shocked that she could take the rail from Peshawar to basically anywhere else. And though the culture on the streets reflected the familiar Muslim-majority culture Zina was familiar with, women were not required to cover themselves as strictly as in Kabul. Moreover, for the first time, Zina saw a movie in a theatre—where she set her eyes on the adorable child actress, Shirley Temple. This was a huge luxury and represented the modernity of Peshawar. It was Shirley Temple's first romantic film of a

---

2 *cheli cha'shan'geh (farsi)*– very pretty

poor girl falling for a wealthy young man. There was identification with the actress, as Zina also had curly locks and a dimple, only her hair was jet black and her dimple was not on her cheeks, but on her chin. Sitting in a dark room with a moving images projected on a screen set the stage for Zina to dream, to imagine a life somewhere else.

In the city, within her aunt Ap Rachel's home, Zina thrived under her care. She taught Zina how to make ancestral dishes with local Indian spices. Rachel was quite a resourceful woman and modeled independence for Zina. Haim would leave on trips for many months, sometimes unable to send any financial help. Rachel would make cheese and sell it for meat to feed her family. In Ap Rachel's home, Zina was growing up quickly. She learned domestic skills at home and focused on her studies, barely paying Rachel's nineteen-year-old son Yehuda any attention. Yehuda was a bright, generous, entrepreneurial young man who was trading as a merchant. He stood out physically from his peers because he wore a wide-brim hat. Zina suspected it was because underneath the hat he was bald.

Rachel's motivations for hosting Zina weren't entirely pure. She predicted that Zina would make excellent marriage material once she grew older and envisioned her as her son's future bride. However, Yehuda saw twelve-year-old Zina as a little sister rather than a love interest. In Ap Rachel's home, Zina was keen, but she did not know that Ap Rachel was a cunning woman quietly planning for the future.

At long last, Zina met her mother's sister Shura and her cousins, Esther, Elusha, Liza, Michael, Raymond, and Chana for the first time. Shura and Ari had moved to Peshawar years prior in search of better economic opportunities and formal education for their children.

Primary education had been free in the Northwest Province since 1912, but only open to girls as of 1944, one year before Zina arrived in Peshawar. Karachi had a bilingual school—Urdu and English. Shura and Ari agreed it was the best option for their children, and they felt that the languages would be useful for their future. Consequently, since they were enrolled in school in another city, Zina could not spend much time with her cousins.

Fortunately, Zina was able to acquire—for the first time in years—formal education in the language of Urdu. In this great city, however, Jews were the minority, the same as in Afghanistan. But in Peshawar, there was an additional religious element: Muslims were the minority within a dominant Hindu state where all religions had to contend with British rule. While Jews were predominantly left out of this religious conflict, tensions simmered, especially as the conflict played out on the broader political stage.

As British delegations met with the Muslim League and the Indian National Congress—two of the largest Indian political parties of the day—to discuss Indian independence and the possibility of a separate Muslim state, the small Jewish population lived in a precarious position. On the one hand, like their Muslim counterparts, they relied on British rule to enforce religious protections for minorities. But unlike the Muslims, who had a segment of government seats held for them and had organized into the Muslim League, the Jews had no outlet to be heard.

On a day-to-day basis, the political machinations of the Muslim League and Gandhi's nonviolent resistance seemed distant for Zina. Though undoubtedly sharp for her age, Zina was too enamored with her new home and school to speculate about politics.

Although British policy was to *divide and rule*—pitting religious groups against each other—Zina's schooling was entirely secular and even co-ed. In this school, Zina did not have to fear corporal punishment for walking out of the classroom during Quran study. Rather, in her school, as part of a national policy toward free and compulsory basic education, children of multiple religions were integrated into the same classroom. She had extended social interaction with Hindu children and other religious groups who were neither the Jews of her home compound nor the Muslims in her home village. Though Zina cherished all of her schoolmates, co-existence in the region was politically tenuous.

Back at home, Hasid would tune into the radio every night to hear the updates on World War II. Indian independence was coming. That much was nearly guaranteed. But the question of Pakistan remained. *Would the Muslim League have the political strength and public support to secure a separate state for India's Muslim population? And for the Jews like Zina, her aunt, and cousins living in Muslim majority provinces, what would this mean for their religious freedom?*

He knew Zina would not quite grasp the political situation until the question of Pakistan moved from newspapers to the streets.

In August 1946, after a British delegation rejected plans to move forward with the creation of a Muslim state carved out of India, the Muslim League called for a rally in Calcutta. They announced Direct Action Day: a general strike in the city. But what could have remained a purely economic boycott became a call for violent action.

Rather than a peaceful strike or a colonial uprising against the British, lower-class Muslim workers attacked and murdered middle-class Hindu shop owners. At first, they targeted anyone who kept their shops open during the general strike but later moved to kill anyone they could find. The Hindus retaliated with slaughter on both sides and became indiscriminate and brutal. Bodies were left to rot in the August heat for days; the dead were shoved into drainage pipes and other water sources.

Direct Action Day lasted more than one day. The violence spilled over into a week, and colonial forces did not step in until the violence had already peaked. The event sparked a chain of violence, sweeping south and west from Calcutta. With every surge of religious violence, refugees fled to where they believed themselves and their families safe. Hindus fled east, further into the sub-continent; Muslims fled west, towards Peshawar and the Afghani border. (Khan, 2017, p.68)

Broadly speaking, Christians and Europeans remained largely safe during the violence. But the Jews in the region, were in an insecure situation, because most of them were ex-pats of Afghanistan and the Soviet Union, successful businessmen who caught the attention of the envious locals. They felt the Jews were taking business opportunities away from them.

The Partition of British India along religious lines of a Hindu-majority India and a Muslim-majority Pakistan was coming, which would end the existing laws of religious freedom.

Benjamin Khafi, who originally came from the same *mahalla* as Zina, had moved to Peshawar some years back and opened a carpet business that quickly became very successful. He rose up to be a community leader for the Jews. By selling carpets to the upper echelons of Peshawar, he developed a good relationship with a local tribal leader, who was also a customer. He warned him that there was an order to kill him and all the Jews in the community. The leader could not stop it, because he was afraid that the locals would kill him for taking the Jews' side. That day, Benjamin went from door to door to warn the Jewish community that an attack was imminent, and they must leave town. To those who could not afford a train ticket out, he bought them a ticket before he boarded himself.

Rachel and her family were on that train. She decided to send Zina back to Kabul, as she did not want the responsibility of another child against the backdrop of such political and religious uncertainty.

Zina understood that with the political situation in flux and travel growing unsafe, it was important for families to migrate *before* they were displaced. Zina said goodbye to Ap Rachel and her cousins and goodbye to her ten months of freedom and education, running from what would soon become a bloody partition and a refugee crisis.

CHAPTER 11

TO THE LAND OF MILK AND HONEY

"Is this another gift from him?" Dora asked Hasid, eyeing a package that had arrived at their housing complex.

"Yes." Hasid responded curtly.

"And I'm guessing another photograph of himself?" The man was in his fifties and had a wife and children in Israel. He was a man of money and influence, and his friends, had misguidedly encouraged him to pursue Zina after seeing twelve-year-old Zina in a community swimming pool. He'd learned her family name and—from there—how to reach her in Kabul. He'd been sending photos of himself to Zina since he saw her in Peshawar along with gifts- generous lengths of fabric- bolts and yards representing every corner of India's textile industry, bold or subtle patterns, embroidered or plain. They sent back each gift unopened.

"And now he is requesting her hand in marriage." Hasid sighed, crossing his arms.

Zina overheard her parents discussing her suitor. *Education and cooking skills, confidence and a taste of freedom, that's what I meant to bring back with me from Peshawar, Not this! Icchh!* The photos and gifts from this old man felt disgusting to her.

Zina vaguely knew that multiple wives for a wealthy man were not that uncommon. She knew that Ap Rachel's father, Amin Kabuli, who owned and operated a grape orchard cultivating wine, had fathered twelve children with three different mothers. Rachel was the youngest of the brood.

"We will ignore his proposal." Dora and Hasid agreed. "He is far too old for Zina *and* already married!" The Shamash family was in a unique position to be able to refuse such displays of wealth. While most Kabuli Jews suffered under increasing economic restrictions, Hasid retained his business with non-Jewish contacts and customers. He could afford to feed his wife and seven children without selling his eldest daughter to a delusional man with lavish gifts. The onslaught of gifts continued for a few years before finally and abruptly, they stopped.

By that time Zina was sixteen and at the age when most Jewish girls of Kabul were already married. Strong, independent Zina had her eye on a different goal: she wanted to move to Israel.

Only a year had passed since Israel declared independence as the official Jewish nation-state. The creation of Israel only heightened Muslim-Jewish tensions. Muslim-majority states faced a double-edged sword regarding their Jewish populations. On the one hand, these governments wanted Jews gone from within their borders, but on the other hand, emigration was a difficult task.

Afghanistan's official policy, for instance, wanted Jews out of the country but would not grant them documents to immigrate to Israel. But Jewish immigration continued out of Afghanistan, the same as it had for decades—mainly illegally.

The Jewish Agency, *Ha-Sochnut*—a non-governmental institution in Jerusalem—made efforts to abolish immigration restrictions imposed on Jews wishing to migrate to Palestine and organized legal and illegal immigration. After the creation of the State of Israel in May 1948, the agency sent emissaries all over the diaspora to collect Jews who wished to immigrate to Israel.

"This is not the time!" Hasid insisted urgently. "I must stay here. There is no work for me in Israel. The only way I can support the family is to trade from here."

When Afghanistan began to allow immigration to Israel, Zina did not doubt that she needed to pursue any opportunity. After all, her paternal grandparents had lived in Tel Aviv since the late 1920s, and there was now an extended family network of aunts, uncles, and cousins she had never met. Zina overheard that her aunt Zipor was moving her family to Israel. She asked her father's permission to travel with her aunt, as she once did to Peshawar. Her parents were divided: Hasid agreed—and Dora did not.

Dora felt that if Zina went, they should all go. She knew from having left her own family in Soviet Uzbek that once you leave, it's nearly impossible to reunite. She had not seen her mother and siblings in over sixteen years. And the tragedy of her sister Shura dying in childbirth pained her greatly. She did not want to miss this chance to move *all* her children out of Afghanistan.

"Please, let me take the children," Dora suggested tentatively as she touched her growing belly with her eighth child. "We might not get another chance." Dora hoped that this child she was carrying would finally be born in a free country. Although tired, her enthusiasm and her will gave her immense strength. She felt compelled to flee the flames of Jewish hatred, fanaticism, and prejudices, before they devoured them all.

Hasid relented. "I will hire a driver to take you all to Israel."

But as more and more Jewish families in their housing complex—and beyond—learned that the Shamash's were immigrating to Israel, they also decided to leave. The hired automobile soon became a hired bus to accommodate the families; thirty people would leave—women and children whose husbands would stay behind to work.

"We can do this. We can. Take as little as possible. We will have a new start." Zina looking after her six younger siblings, helped them pack their bags. Each child would carry a small sack of clothing onto the bus. The larger sacks were strapped to the roof with rails helping big items stay in place. Families crammed into the bus seats with the youngest children on laps while the older children crowded the aisles, using their sacks of clothes as seat cushions. Children crouched knee to knee, and the women bumped shoulders. Between the folds of their skirts, they clutched bags of dried fruit and nuts. In their hands, canteens of water. It was noisy and it was hot. People dripped with sweat. Unbathed bodies permeated the air with a tangy foul stench like cooked onions. Windows slid open letting in the dry air. The bus seemed to burst at the seams with expectation.

There was a straight route of 2020 kilometers west from Kabul to Tehran. However, the bus needed to skirt around provinces that were hostile to Jews. There were long stretches of desert and twisting, unpaved, cratered roads that wound over and around dusty mountains. The bus dashed full speed, swerving first to the right then to the left, its fenders rattling loudly as it streaked over the underbrush, wheels crunching the gravel and crushing stones, dead snakes, and broken branches.

The first stop was Herat, followed by Mashhad, and other prominent Jewish towns towards Tehran. It was rough and uncomfortable, but Zina only felt joy. While the children rejoiced in expected freedom, the older women breathed in their children's hope while tamping their fear. The older women prayed and worried that marauders would cause an accident on the road or rob and kill the passengers. No one would ever know what became of them on such deserted roads.

For the most part, the trip went smoothly. The bus would stop every few days at designated Jewish families along the way who opened their doors to feed and house the travelers. Not every town or village they passed would have kosher food or be amenable to Jews, but when they did stop, they were embraced by warm hospitality. In each town, everyone on board the bus disembarked, stretched their numb and shaky legs and divided themselves up to stay with families and get some sleep. There they bathed, changed their clothes, restocked their food, and rested in good company. This was their new rhythm, re-boarding the bus, crowding together in hope as they continued west to Israel.

One day when a message had already been sent ahead that the travelers were coming, the bus rattled to a stop, making horrible sounds. "What happened?" Zina asked her mother.

"I think the bus has broken down." Just as they had grown to trust their supporters along the way, they had become accustomed to trusting the bus.

"What will we do?" Zina looked at her mother.

"We wait," Dora said, nodding to Zina to look after her siblings.

"Good thing it's springtime, and not too hot," Zina pointed out, always the positive one.

The children amused themselves with their games while the adults talked amongst themselves, still fearful of robbers. Some sat on their bags of clothing, and others moved around the bus to stay in the cooler shadows throughout the day's heat.

The passengers had to wait six hours until another bus came barreling past them, heading back to Kabul. When it stopped, the families pooled their money and paid the new bus driver to take a message to Kabul: send *another* bus for the stranded families.

Their journey was no longer a direct trip to Israel. Now, the bus's final destination was the Mehrabad Airport in Iran's capital Tehran. Iran had a good relationship with Israel and was the second Muslim-majority country—Turkey being the first—to officially recognize the State of Israel. Israel even had a delegation serving as an embassy in Tehran. The city became a waystation for Jews heading to Israel, where the Israeli government-chartered planes to take Jewish refugees to Lod Airport in Tel Aviv. Iran was an ally in Israel's early years. It benefitted from this alliance, as they were more than willing to supply Israel with oil, especially as Israel's early years were marked by an Arab boycott severely limiting imports, exports, and economic growth.

"Look, what a modern city!" Zina told her siblings as the bus arrived and finally parked. The family glimpsed the capital city of a near-eastern country that possessed a strong eye toward Western ideas of progress. Pulsing with cars clogging the streets, they knew within that noise was access to religious and secular higher education, and a robust infrastructure supporting the civilian airport now hosting them. For the first time, they saw traffic lights, lamp posts, and asphalt-paved roads. They were in awe as they thought: *We are in the richest country in the world.*

"Peshawar was not as modern as Tehran," Zina stated, her eyes widening in amazement. She gently pushed her little sister Tamar off her lap so she could wholly take in her new surroundings.

Although Tehran was a modern city, it was not built to even temporarily house an influx of refugees. Transit camps dotted the city's outskirts, housing Afghani Jews alongside Iranian and Iraqi Jews with limited sanitation and resources. The Israeli government chartered planes, but not every Jewish refugee could afford the plane ticket. If you or your family could not afford the expense, you had to wait in the transit camps until the Israeli government arranged your travel. Some individuals and families waited for months.

Yet, the only way out of Afghanistan was to immigrate to Israel. Hasid had bigger plans for his family and did not want to use Israel's resources for tickets to Israel because the long plan was to eventually move the family to America. Although he did not share his idea with anyone at the time, Hasid was influenced by the Abrams' lifestyle and the opportunities for Jews that they shared over their many years of being hosted by the Shamash's.

Dora was relieved they could fly away from this life and end this ordeal. Zina knew how fortunate they were as the family had money from Hasid's continued success as a merchant, and before the family left on the bus, Dora had sewn gold coins into their clothes. Zina was so grateful that all eight of them could purchase tickets, thanks to her parents' prudence.

Zina sat in the plane with her nose pushed up against the window, eyes fixed on the tarmac. She pressed her fingers against the glass window, her breath quick with anticipation. Commercial flying was still relatively new, so it was a first-class luxury experience designed for the wealthy elites in fine dresses and pressed suits. It was not meant for refugees coming off a twenty-one-day bus ride. No one on this plane had ever seen a metal flying machine before. The younger siblings were bursting with curiosity and pressed any button and lever they saw, curious to see what the controls did.

The plane was rolled down the runway groaning, belching, and jerking from side to side. Then Dora watched the windblown landscape flash by as the plane ascended into the air. *We are as free as we have ever been.* Dora and Zina exchanged knowing looks mid-air. They could throw off their *chadors*, practice Judaism without fear, and praise G-d for the start of their new lives.

When the plane touched the ground with all kinds of metallic bumps and jumps, landing in an open field at Lod Airport everyone in the entire plane clapped.

CHAPTER 12

FROM SHAMASH TO ABRAHAM: WELCOME TO ISRAEL

Hasid's grandfather, Abraham, was a merchant who traveled between the cities of Herat, Mashhad, Samarkand, and Marv. He would arrive in these cities on his horse or donkey, stopping in other smaller centers. One of the places where he regularly stopped was a small town named Yusef Abad. Many other Jews also traveled the same path, and in the course of a number of years, Yusef Abad became a known stopping point for the Jews. Eventually, Abraham and other Jews decided to establish a small synagogue there. Abraham became the caretaker of the synagogue—the *Shamash* in Hebrew and assisted those who came to pray there.

The name "Shamash" became a nickname, and Abraham was called Abraham Shamash. Over the years, the nickname became a family name—Shamash. When the Shamash's moved to Israel, they decided to change the family name to Abraham, in honor of their grandfather Abraham and the start of their new lives. New name, new life.

"You will go over there. That way," an officer stated, directing the women toward the resettlement camps. They approached Dora and her family, but she vehemently refused to be taken to one of these camps. Immigrants who arrived without family already living in Israel to take them in—many Shoah survivors without family—lived in *ma'abarot*, tent cities sponsored and maintained by the Israeli government, until long-lasting solutions could be implemented. Arriving Jews at the ports were met with government officials for intake into these *ma'abarot*.

We did not leave the backward country of Afghanistan to now live in a tent, Dora thought, upset that their ordeal was not over. She was determined to upgrade her life and her children's lives too. Thankfully, Hasid sent her with enough money to set them up in their new homeland, and his family, already living in Israel, awaited their arrival. She was able to straighten out their situation and move on to their family reunion. Sadly though, Dora had none of her immediate family in Israel—and she always longed for them. Manny, her long-lost uncle whom she'd hoped to see had somehow just vanished from the family.

The Shamash immigrants, now with a new surname Abraham, were met by Zina's paternal grandparents, Chana and Agajan, who were delighted to receive the tired crew they had never met before. Since there were simply too many children to fit into the grandparents' single-room apartment in the Tel Aviv neighborhood of Florentin, Zina and her siblings were divided up among their grandparents and aunts: Miriam, Bachmal, and Biti—their father's sisters. The first few nights, the family was separated and slept on the floor of relatives until their uncle Shlomo found them a two-bedroom walk-up apartment close to them with a terrace facing the bustling Rehov Herzl.

The bedrooms were tiny, only meant for sleeping, not lounging, plus they had a small living room that was very plain and bare, with only enough space for a dining table and a sofa. But they were excited to discover they had their own bathroom. The apartment had the basic amenities, except for a refrigerator which was a rare commodity. "*Dadeh* will send money for us to buy a refrigerator," said Dora and added with relief, "No more pee pee into a bowl in the middle of the night or cold runs outside." Although the living arrangements were cramped, all eight slept in the apartment with some ingenuity.

In the master bedroom, Moshe shared the bed with his mother. Since Moshe was male and thus the favored child, he had that privilege while the girls slept in trundle beds, head to toe: Tamar and Zina, Zipora and Hannah, Rosa on the floor, and Yafa in a tiny cot. No one had the luxury of sleeping in their own bed. Surviving peacefully required cooperation and closeness.

Though the girls shared the same bedroom, they all had very different personalities that suited their role within the household. Yafa had a natural knack for being a caretaker, and was always the responsible one, particularly for Tamar. Tamar, the younger sister, was the complete opposite of her older sister. She was social, and loved putting on her mother's lipstick.

Every night, after Yafa put Tamar to bed, she stayed up late taking care of household chores and chatting with her older sisters. But every night without fail, Tamar would wake up in the middle of the night hungry, and would nudge Yafa from her sleep to fix her something to eat. Yafa, tired of being disturbed night after night, came up with a brilliant plan. She kept a few pieces of bread under her pillow, just in case Tamar woke up hungry.

"Yafa, get up!" Tamar nudged Yafa from her sleep. "I'm hungry. Can you make me something to eat?"

"Oooofffff, Tamar, not again. Here... I have some bread." She shoved her hand under the pillow.

"Let me just grab it!"

"*Regah[1]! Loh[2]!* Yelped Yafa in Hebrew. "Don't touch it!"

"*Mah karah[3]?*"

"There's an *achbar[4]*! It's already eaten a hole in the bread!"

"Icchhhh.... A mouse!

"I guess the mouse was hungry too. I'll make you something else to eat."

"*Todah[5]* Yafa! You're the best!"

Dora assigned all the girls jobs with precision and accuracy, channeling her past life when she was the factory's bookkeeper back in Russia. "Zina, you'll be my helper in the kitchen and will help sewing the clothes, and Yafa, you can help me with your younger sisters."

Dora recognized that Zina was very good with her hands and had a knack for being a seamstress. And Zina perfectly sewed all their clothes by hand, including their undergarments.

The homes were close enough together for the grandparents to host the children in their home on Saturday night after *Havdalah*– the

---

1 *Regah (Hebrew)*– wait
2 *Loh (Hebrew)*– no
3 *Mah karah (Hebrew)*– what happened?
4 *Achbar (Hebrew)*– mouse
5 *Todah (Hebrew)*– thank you

closing ritual at the end of Shabbat. The grandparents were *shomer-Shabbat* and continued to wear traditional Bukharan head coverings and dresses. But the rest of Tel Aviv surprised the Abraham girls in its diversity of Jewish observance—the family had expected a Jewishly-observant state. Instead, it was divided.

Dora wanted to protect her children from the non-kosher world. "Shield your eyes. Do not even look in the direction of the slaughterhouse," Dora urged. Across the street from the apartment was a slaughterhouse for pigs and cows. Blood would regularly flow into the streets. There had been an influx of Shoah survivors, many of whom were secular Jews who considered eating pig a delicacy. It was one of the many reasons Dora insulated her children from anyone who was not Bukharan, to ensure that they would keep Jewish laws and customs. *My family has been persecuted for hundreds of years, and we had to run from country to country because we are Yahudis. My father was sent to the gulag to die because he was rich and Jewish. All this did not happen for us to come to Israel and assimilate.* Dora thought to herself.

Yet Israel was already an eclectic mix of Judaism that mirrored the diversity and observance of the world's Jewish people. For the first three years of Israel's existence as a state, upwards of 200,000 Jews immigrated yearly. Immigrants varied in national origin. Israel's culture shape-shifted to accommodate its new population; for the most part, the family felt at home. They quickly assimilated into Israeli society.

It's no surprise that the majority of the state's budget went toward the military or resettlement. In the early years, the government relied on American aid, donations from world Jewry, and, after 1952, reparations from Germany. Even immigrants like the Abrahams, those with family and a stable place to live, could not escape these larger economic concerns dominating the country's future.

"Oooofffff......this line is so long!" Yafa complained to her sisters as they waited in the market where food was rationed out. Zina looked around at the lines of people waiting for food, shrugged her shoulders, and nodded in agreement. Food rationing was an exact science of 1600 calories per day per person, and the Ministry of Rationing and Supply created baskets of essentials. These baskets could only be purchased through government-approved stores unless one was willing to enter the black market.

Zina replied, "Looks like the whole country is here with a coupon book for our six-lire ration per month." After the establishment of Israel, a country desperately poor and reeling from a grueling War of Independence, it absorbed an enormous influx of newcomers. Israel had to institute an emergency rationing plan for the distribution of food, as well as many other goods and commodities.

Zina was aware that their fortune had changed and continued, "Still, Israel is the best place on earth." The sisters nodded in agreement. They understood that despite the hardship they were fortunate to be there. They were getting an education—and here they did not fear being Jewish.

"They are giving out sugar, butter, bread, and powdered milk." Rosa chimed in.

"Add that to the food packages from America and we'll make do." Anonymous Zionist American benefactors sent food to Israel in support of the newly formed state.

One person who helped them a lot was their Bobo Agajan, who woke up every morning before the sun rose, and headed to the wholesale market at Rehov Aliya to source fresh fruits and vegetables to sell. The market was bustling with activity, and Bobo spent hours bargaining with vendors for the best possible prices.

After carefully selecting his produce, Bobo would load them into a handcart and trudge back to his apartment. Once back home, he would lovingly arrange the fruits and vegetables in a neat pile on the footpath outside his house. He would then wait patiently for customers to come by. Agajan had a long beard that gave him the look of kindness and wisdom and a spark in his eyes that made him quite popular among his customers. Occasionally, Zina would drop by his apartment at the end of the day to say hello and check if there was any produce to spare.

When they came home with food, the first person to be fed was Moshe, then the girls. It was understood and never questioned that Dora divided herself into two uneven halves: to Moshe and her six daughters.

Breakfast and lunch were the same--bread, butter, and sugar. For dinner, Dora prepared a large pot of rice with chicken that she cut into tiny pieces to feed the entire family.

"No one will leave our table hungry... or messy." All the sisters smiled as they worked together to clean up. Zipora picked up the dishes, Rosa washed them, Hannah dried them, and Tamar was tasked with washing the floor.

There is always work to be done. The apartment was kept spotless because of Dora's Russian influences of discipline, precision, and perfection. No one was allowed to—or even dared to -just lounge around. Everyone had to be useful.

The girls enjoyed their freedom and, for the first time, received a formal education. Dora, highly educated herself, knew the value of education. She was now an older woman in a new country bogged down with daily chores and unable to go to school, so she urged her daughters to teach her Hebrew. Soon enough,

Bukharian was eclipsed by Hebrew in the home. In the meantime, her neighbors would stop by and ask her to read and write letters in Russian for them, from family still stuck in the Soviet Union.

When the girls first entered school, most of their teachers were of Ashkenazi descent and viewed these girls with long hair and darker skin as otherworldly. There were some prejudices against Mizrachi Jews, who were considered uncultured and uncouth. The schools that the Abraham girls attended forced them to cut their long hair and treat their scalps in case they carried lice.

Predictably, conflicts also arose between Yishuv Jews, who were those living in Israel before the official creation of the state, and new immigrants—almost one-third of them being Shoah survivors. Jews from Arab or Central Asian countries, Asia, Africa, and the United States were thrown into this mix. Everyone came with their own version of Judaism: secular and Orthodox, as well as Ashkenazi, Sephardic, and Mizrahi. This added to the tension.

Another option to escape some of the economic hardship on families was the kibbutz, where young adults would live and work in small communities, primarily in agriculture. Those living on kibbutzim became known as "children of the cream" as they had access to fresh milk and eggs and did not have to rely on government-rationed dry and powdered foods.

This was also a great opportunity to receive an education, learn a trade, and hone one's Hebrew. Zipora and Rosa went to a kibbutz for their education. Yafa was considered too valuable to the household, especially for her skill in taking care of the younger children, particularly since Dora was nearing the final months of another pregnancy.

Rosa, who was twelve years old, was a bit of a wayward child, always taking risks, wandering off by herself, and needed some discipline and attention. There was a youth village, a boarding high school, in Petah Tikva called *mosad*, aimed at newly immigrated children from religious homes who were at risk and needed more support than the traditional school system offered. Although Rosa was technically far too young, Dora enrolled Rosa into the *mosad* as "Yafa Abraham" on her paperwork, posing as a fourteen-year-old. Rosa proceeded into the youth village as if she were the same age as the other girls. She quickly became known as Yafa-Rosa when it became clear that she did not respond when called just Yafa.

A special teacher, Morah[6] Sabo, took notice of Rosa's extraordinary hard work and fearlessness. She was a Shoah survivor and had immigrated to Israel with no family, as they had all perished. Rosa flourished in the *mosad* and was dearly trusted by the headmaster, who assigned Rosa to be the caretaker of her own children. During the school year, when there were occasional vacation breaks and the students would return home, Rosa knew Morah Sabo had no family to return to. She was so beloved by Rosa that Rosa stayed with her during her vacation time, and they forever bonded.

Dora was in labor. Her eighth child was about to be born. There was no calling in a midwife, no home birth. Instead Zina called a taxi and took her mother to the hospital, where a medical doctor delivered the baby girl. Dora named her final child *Bracha:* blessing.

It would be ten years before Hasid left Afghanistan and saw his wife and met Bracha for the first time.

---

6 *Morah (Hebrew)–* teacher

CHAPTER 13

MARRIAGE MINDED IN ISRAEL

" *Bi'zaaaaahn[1]*," Zina said in amazement, "*Ma'chineh[2]*?" Zina sputtered, looking at her cousin Yehuda who stood in front of a brand-new Chevy. She couldn't believe her eyes. Zina had never seen such luxury. It had been years since she last saw her cousin in Peshawar. She'd been a little girl at the time and Yehuda had seemed so much older to her, and of course she'd had no interest in boys at the time. But years later, reuniting in Israel as a

---

1 *Bi'zaaaaahn (Judeo farsi)*– an expression for amazement
2 *Ma'chineh (farsi)*– car

young lady and Yehuda as a bachelor, made her see him in a new light that surprised her.

"I bought myself a car!" Yehuda said, a proud smile taking over his usually modest features. Most Israelis didn't have the kind of resources required to purchase a car, let alone immigrants, and yet Yehuda said, "You know I like *cha'shan'ghe* things and I worked hard to get it."

Zina blushed, burying her head, smiling slightly. She thought to herself how charming Yehuda was, and couldn't believe that it was her own cousin she was falling for.

Prior to Yehuda's arrival in Israel, he had sent word from Bombay to his mother Rachel in Tel Aviv that he "had found his bride," an Iraqi woman. But his mother replied he would *not* marry a woman "outside of our community." So instead, she hatched a plan. Rachel told Yehuda, "Come to Israel and see if you find someone from our people. If you do not find a wife after your stay in Israel, you may return to Bombay with my blessings for marriage."

Dutifully, Yehuda traveled from Bombay to Tel Aviv. While back in Bombay, Yehuda's "fiancé" joyfully shared with her family and friends that she was engaged to be married. Rachel got wind of this and was unhappy that this news was spreading, and maybe ruining the opportunity for Yehuda and Zina to come together.

Rachel still had her eye on Zina as a wife for her son, and now that Yehuda and Zina were both at marriageable age— Zina then nineteen and Yehuda twenty-seven—it was time to propose the match. So rather than pressing Zina on her son, Rachel cleverly devised a plan. She arranged a welcome party for Yehuda and invited several eligible women to the house whom were not as pretty as Zina. Some of these women Zina knew and was friends with, some were cousins and other family members, but all had been hand-selected by Rachel to make sure that Yehuda chose Zina.

Zina looked at her suitor and his car, impressed. Yehuda was handsome and well-dressed, elegant in a suit and tie, Yehuda's style was highly unusual in Israel, where the common dress was a T-shirt and pants with socks peeking through leather sandals.

"*Bi'yah*[3]," Yehuda said, "Let me take you for a drive."

Yehuda had already impressed Zina in small and impactful ways like when Yehuda would visit Zina at their apartment, he would always bring some gift. For the family, he would usually bring lots of fruit. And whenever the sisters would bicker, Yehuda would intervene, always the peacemaker.

So Zina agreed immediately to go for a ride, as she always felt safe and warm around Yehuda. He helped her into the passenger seat. She enjoyed his company as they drove off, but her mind was also traveling, eager to see where this new road between them would go.

Yehuda zipped past a café where a bunch of giggly young women were sitting outside, enjoying the sun and chit-chatting away. The scene reminded Zina of her new friends. It felt profound to her that she finally had the freedom to do something as simple as form bonding friendships with other young women. She was thankful for her friends that helped her bridge her old life with her new in Tel Aviv. She fondly recalled how her friends were always helping her with her Hebrew, which eventually landed her a job in a shoe store. Interacting with customers gave her more confidence in her Hebrew and helped her feel more connected to her new home.

Many of her friends were Bukharan with similar backgrounds and shared languages. Some of these friends had been

---

3 *Bi'yah (farsi)*– come

in Israel for years. Others were recent immigrants like Zina. But, by coincidence, her closest friends were two women named Shoshana. *I know many friendships may naturally fade with age, but I know both Shoshanas will be with me for life. We share and help each other with everything.*

Zina was very striking with her black curly hair, big almond eyes, and full lips—a young, darker version of Sofia Loren. She'd expanded her social life to include possible suitors, some within the family and some with family friends. Even with increased freedom in Israel, marriage was far from a free-for-all. She knew that the man she married must be approved by her parents and her Bibi and Bobo. He must be from a similar background, either a family member or a long-standing friend of the family.

What Zina did not know was that Dora would send out Moshe to spy on her. Dora and Moshe had a special kinship, sleeping in the same room, even sharing the same oxford shoes.

"Moshe, you are the man of the house. You must protect your sisters, especially Zina. Many *chostogor*[4] want her. I want to know who they are and where she is going. Go... go and follow her, and report back to me." Moshe, who was all but twelve years old, would follow Zina, hiding behind trees and buildings like a secret agent for the Mossad and dutifully reported back to his mother.

As Yehuda drove, he pointed out a few notable city sites. Zina remembered seeing some of the same places when she rode with a cab driver she'd met at a wedding. In typical Israeli custom, weddings were relatively informal. Guests did not dress up for the occasion, and frequently invitations were open to friends of guests. Just a year or so before, Zina's friends were invited to a Bukharan

---

4 *Chostogor (farsi)*– bachelor

wedding. They had urged her to come and join them as it would be a girls' night out. Zina obliged, and it was there that a tall, handsome blond man spotted Zina from across the dance floor. He, too, was Bukharan but had emigrated years before Zina, and was a taxi driver who owned his own taxi. The man approached Zina, made some small talk with her, and offered her and her friends a ride home in his shiny taxi.

But I did not realize, she reminded herself with compassion, *that when he dropped me off at my home, he would remember where I lived.* He often came around to their home and waited for Zina to go out of the building. She would get into the front of his taxi and sit next to him, unlike his fares who would sit in the back. She felt so free and worldly. Initially she was thrilled, but she did not know that her close relatives were keeping an eye from a distance. Nor did she know that another admirer was also lurking in the background and watching her with the mysterious man.

For months she rode with him until that one day she stepped out of his cab, and her relative and this other admirer were there. Zina flinched as a horrible image came rushing in. *Stop*, she told herself. Zina tried not to recall how they ganged up on the cab driver, dragged him out of his car, and beat him up. *My family thought they were protecting me. They feared that he would do something inappropriate and take advantage of me.*

Dora watched the whole event unfold from her terrace. As Zina walked into the apartment, Dora pounced on her. "You must tell me who you are with at all times! Never get into a car with someone I don't know!" Zina had no time to defend herself from the smacks around her head. From then on, Zina told her mother about all her dates and she never entered his cab again.

Zina noticed Yehuda was navigating to a less-busy area of Tel Aviv. Perhaps he had a plan, and they were going somewhere more romantic. She felt a fire inside of her. He had quirky qualities about him in nearly everything he did, such as how he would turn the steering wheel. Yehuda would turn the steering wheel from the bottom of the wheel, moving his hands inches at a time. As he drove, he would suck his teeth from the side of his mouth and spit. Nonetheless, Zina found him charming and all his quirks endearing.

Yehuda had pulled over in a less busy, quieter part of Tel Aviv. Were they to have a meaningful conversation now? They looked at each other. Yehuda wasn't like Zina remembered him. *Perhaps I didn't even remember him well at all.* She laughed to herself. *When I lived in Peshawar, there were plenty of things more interesting to me than an older man—school, helping Ap Rachel around the house, and making friends my own age.*

Now I see Yehuda as . . . my future husband. Zina reflected on all they had been through to get to this point, thankful the two had decided to date. It felt right when they were reunited and conversed at the welcome party; it was both familiar and new at the same time, comfortable but exciting. She also liked that he was gentle and respectful with his mother and other women at the party.

Yehuda started to exit the driver's seat. "What are we doing?" Zina asked, surprised.

"I'm teaching you to drive," he said simply.

"*Neh, neh,*" Zina replied instantly, "We can't." She could not believe that this dapper gentleman was suggesting that she take the wheel. It was unheard of for a woman of her background to drive a car. It was considered vulgar and would cheapen her status among her peers. However, this was not Yehuda's line of thought.

"*Chi'wah*[5]?" Yehuda asked, flicking his head and hand.

Always curious to learn something new and develop herself, Zina got a feel for the gas and brake pedals and the sturdy large steering wheel. *I can do this*, she thought, feeling rebellious. Yehuda gave instructions while Zina listened, her attention full bore. But still, Zina was new to operating a car, so her reaction times were just a bit too slow and confused. With a panicked squeal, Zina stepped on the gas pedal instead of the brake pedal just as Yehuda's new vehicle made contact with the back bumper of the car in front of them.

"*Ibi*[6]!" Zina gushed immediately, panicking and hopping out of the driver's seat to assess the damage.

"It's okay, okay," Yehuda assured her, calm and amused. He briefly spoke with the driver of the car that Zina hit, then the two of them made their way home with him behind the wheel and Zina sitting sheepishly in the passenger's seat.

When Zina got home, she told her mother about the minor disaster. "There's only one solution," she replied, "You have to marry him. You ruined his car." Zina joined her mother in laughing, but neither was genuinely joking. Sure enough, after only a month of courting, Yehuda announced to his mother that he had chosen Zina as his bride. Rachel, of course, approved, and so did Zina's parents. It was a *shidduch*—a perfect match.

Secretly, Rachel sent word to her son's former fiancé in India that Yehuda was getting married to a woman in Israel. As a consolation, Rachel financially compensated this woman so that she could leave India, since Zina and Yehuda would return to Bombay as husband and wife.

---

5   *Chi'wah (Judeo farsi)* – why?
6   *Ibi (Judeo farsi)* – a word for surprise

Zina's tired hands finished the final tucks on her wedding dress in the very early morning of a crisp day right in the middle of winter, January 1953. She had sourced some silk charmeuse and lace fabric for her wedding dress near her home on Jaffa Street, which was lined with fabric stores. It was a simple, modest, sweetheart neckline dress with a bodice cinched at the waist and flared out. The sleeves were made from lace with pearl closures at the wrist and back of the dress. She collected her thoughts and smiled at how she had done so much sewing for others, but these threads were for her big day.

It wasn't just her big day, but an important affair for their families. Since family was marrying family, and Yehuda's family came from a very comfortable lifestyle, other family members coat-tailed their celebrations onto their wedding.

She touched the silk, letting its smoothness soothe her nerves. Soon, nearly seven hundred people gathered together to celebrate Zina's marriage to Yehuda, but it was so much more than that. Zina's uncle, Shlomo, was to marry a Bukharan named Tamar. They could not afford a lavish wedding and so two weddings combined. The weddings took place at the Namal of Tel Aviv, a sparkling waterfront on the Mediterranean Sea.

The wedding date also coincided with Moshe's long-awaited *bar mitzvah*, the family's first male coming-of-age celebration. During the day, the sun was still high in the January sky, and the family celebrated Moshe's *bar mitzvah*. Dora stood proud, while hiding her sadness, that once again Hasid was missing the major memorable events in their lives. Hasid could not extricate himself from his businesses in Afghanistan and make the arduous trip.

The celebration was a whirl of painted silk colors from a kaleidoscope. The older men were dressed in traditional Bukharan costumes: brightly colored and heavily embroidered coats with large flat-top skull caps. Similarly, the older women donned colorful gowns of a lighter fabric, with their heads covered in sheer silk scarves. These women also kept the tradition of slapping the *doira*—a large leather tambourine from Bukhara with metal rings on the inside. They extracted a melodic ringing drumbeat as they circled the guests.

It was a collision of old and new. The younger generation had already been ensconced into Israeli society. Some men wore white shirts and large-brimmed hats, and those enrolled in the army came in their IDF uniform and caps. You could tell the workers from the business men based on their hats. The workers, like the cab drivers and delivery men, wore caps. The women married to the merchants could afford fitted silk dresses, although the individual style was not yet commonplace in the new socialist-formed country.

Men and women mingled in the hall while Zina was in another room, getting ready and receiving blessings from her grandparents. Bobo Agajan placed his hands on her head and blessed her. Zina, in turn, kissed his hand as a sign of respect.

Dora soon pulled her daughter aside: "Zina, I have one piece of advice for you: wherever your husband goes, you go. Never let him leave you." Dora held her hand and looked intently into Zina's eyes. Dora had become embittered over rarely seeing Hasid. She had chosen her children and the opportunity to live in a community with other Jews over the stilted life imposed upon them in Afghanistan. This predicament left her perpetually frustrated. So, the soundest advice she could give her daughter—who was moving to Bombay with Yehuda—was to always stay by his side.

Yehuda, whose desire to be fastidiously well groomed meant that he was perpetually tardy. He was at the barber shop and arrived late—even for his wedding. While everyone was pacing around waiting for him, he was taking his sweet dear time getting ready. It was never a question that he wouldn't show. When he finally came, he carried himself like an ambassador—self-assured, elegant, and greeting everyone one at a time.

The weddings proceeded just before sunset, each couple taking their place under the *chuppah* for the traditional blessings and finishing with shouts of "Mazal Tov!"

Typical Bukharan cuisine was served, family style and plentiful. The table overflowed with variations of *pilov* with candied orange rinds, dried cherries, pistachios and almond toppings, as well as *ghoshghijha,* which is baked meat in a dough, *non toki,* a round flat bread covered in black sesame seeds, and a multitude of tangy salads. They ended the meal with fragrant black *choi* and fresh watermelon.

"Well, Zina, what do you think?"

The couples, Shlomo and Tamar, and Yehuda and Zina took their honeymoon together: a driving tour of Israel. The first stop was north to Haifa- the largest seaport in Israel, where it was a pleasure driving through the tree-lined streets that were much wider than the roads in Tel Aviv.

They wandered the shuk's[7] narrow lanes, smelling cantaloupes and eggplants and took in the fruits and vegetables displayed in rows of primary colors under the blistering sun, assaulted by loud hagglers and the overhanging stench of raw fish.

Yehuda especially loved action; he loved commerce and loved to people-watch. He stared at the traders enveloped in their theatrics.

They strolled along *Mosheva HaGermanit*—the German colony established in Ottoman Palestine by Lutheran Germans who settled there to prepare for Jesus's promised return.

---

7 *Shuk (Hebrew)*- market

"I have lived in Israel for almost three years but only experienced Tel Aviv!" This country is full of life and filled with our people.

Yehuda chimed in, "I have experienced even *less* of the country."

What they saw together was an Israel that was still changing, finding its own identity, and learning to be self-sufficient. The country was grappling with food production for its growing population, harnessing technology to make the arid land easier to live on and produce food.

"I feel like this honeymoon is both a hello and goodbye tour," Zina pronounced.

"What do you mean?" Tamar asked.

"Well, I am seeing new things as if I am new to Israel, and I am saying 'Shalom' as I will be moving to Bombay with Yehuda for his family gem business."

"You will be newly brave in Bombay!"

"As always, I embrace new destinations," Zina stated, aware that her travels and moves had colored her life with culture and charm.

Dora & Hasid
Soviet Uzbek, early 1930's

Zina at twelve years old, Peshawar 1945;
Top row: Zina, Yehuda, and Yehuda's sister Tamar;
Sitting: Haim, Rachel, Mayer's wife Tamar and Mayer

Left to right sitting: Zina, Tamar, Hanna, and Dora;
Standing: Rosa, Zipora, Yafa, and Moshe
Afghanistan, 1947

Left to right: Zipora, Moshe, Dora, and Zina
Israel, 1949

Zina and Yehuda wedding photo
Israel, 1953

Zina in Bombay
India 1955

Zina at the top of the stairs with her sisters
Forest Hills, New York, 1960's

Zina's grandparent's one hundred-year-old
birthday celebration, Chana and Agajan Abramoff
Israel, 1963

Dora in Soviet Uzbek 1966; Sitting in the center

Zina and Yehuda in silk brocade *jomah's*,
customarily worn on holidays and celebrations
New York 2012

CHAPTER 14

BRAVE IN BOMBAY

"This is where Duke Ellington sat!" Yehuda commented to Zina with pride. The couple spent their evenings with friends at the Taj Mahal Hotel, drinking chai- black tea with cardamom and steamed milk, and conversing with other foreigners.

I am happy here, and even Yehuda's business is prosperous here. Zina mused: *I am finally enjoying the life I dreamed of as a young girl and I'm no longer a religious target, like back in Afghanistan.* Yet she knew that wasn't true for everyone.

Although there were long-established Jewish populations in India—predominantly the Bene Israel, the Cochin, and Baghdadi—these groups of Jews were still Indians by birth. After the Indian partition, many Indian Jews immigrated to Israel. But the Indian Jews who stayed faced a shift in their socio-economic status post-Indian independence. Under the

British divide-and-rule principle, Jews had some preferential treatment, where the British awarded Jews more access to formal education and additional economic opportunities. Indian Jews, lacked the numbers to pose a threat to the British Empire, and would remain loyal subjects. But with Indian independence, many Jews immigrated due to the precarity of their position in Indian society. The Jews who remained lost their privileged status and wound up on the fringes of the economy.

Zina and Yehuda, fortunately, were not part of these groups; they were foreign Jews and were not bound to the shifts in politics and economics the same way Indian Jews were. For one, due to the success of Yehuda's multiple businesses, they could enjoy Indian culture and entertainment.

After all, the 1950s was the Golden Age of Indian cinema. Since throwing off British rule and suffering through the violent aftermath of partition, creativity took hold, and the arts flourished. Zina and Yehuda would frequent Indian movie theaters, taking in socio-political dramas that were shown internationally and received world acclaim. Zina knew every day how lucky she was. Her life had grown safe, comfortable, and—above all—*fulfilled*.

Jawaharlal Nehru, India's first Prime Minister—a leader in Indian independence and a disciple of Gandhi—faced several economic struggles upon taking office. While determined to end the caste system, Nehru inherited an underdeveloped economy and a dense population. The citizens of Bombay were not as prosperous as the film industry. Poverty plagued the city.

Despite that, Indians always rejoiced in the colorful festival of Holi, also known as the "festival of love." On this day, people came together, let loose, celebrated love and playfully threw brightly colored powder in the air and immersed themselves in head-to-toe color. Zina and Yehuda partook in the fun aspects of the Hindu practices in this holiday by visiting a local festival. It was a massive celebration including women in lush, iridescent saris, pulsating peacocks, regal elephants, and white cows roaming where they pleased. Nonstop food stalls dotted the entire campground.

The vibrancy of colors brought in a lot of positivity, and Holi, the festival of colors, was a day of rejoicing. At the festival, a bucket of what seemed like a punch was at one of the stalls. Yehuda and Zina helped themselves to a ladle of this punch, which they later learned was an edible mixture made from the buds, leaves, and flowers of the female cannabis plant, *bhang*.

"Yehuda, I think I see monkeys in the trees," Zina said in a reverie. There were no monkeys in the trees, but by the organ grinders and as part of their act.

"Zina, my head is spinning," Yehuda said, holding his head in his hands.

Days later, Zina was still feeling strange and it was concerning to her. *Should I still be feeling weird days after I drank that bhang?* She thought to herself. Feeling nauseous and tired all the time, while having trouble sleeping, she decided to visit the doctor to see what was wrong. She visited a British doctor who'd come to India to get his medical degree and stayed on to work at the private hospital called *The King Edward Memorial* hospital. The doctor ran some tests and delivered the news to Zina, "Madam, you are pregnant." Zina was shocked that she got pregnant so quickly and felt a bit scared. It was too soon for her. She was just starting a new life, full of possibilities, comfort, and freedoms. The last thing she wanted was to be tied down again.

Zina walked home towards Queens Road to their three-story walk-up apartment building in a daze, barely noticing the cow manure and discarded mango rinds littering the dirt roads and baking in the sun. The sticky scent of saffron, curry, and damp earth laced the breeze entering into Zina's nostrils and making her queasy. Slowly and pensively, she climbed the steps to her apartment. Yehuda was sitting in the living room in the reading chair waiting for her return. Zina shared the news. Yehuda was so happy at the news, that it melted away all her fears.

"I'm happy to be a father and I will take care of you and get you a nurse to make it easier for you once the baby is born." Zina was relieved that her husband was so understanding and supportive. Initially, she was scared of the responsibility that she didn't feel ready for, but now she was looking forward to the new chapter in their lives. She was determined to be a good mother and to give her baby the best education possible. Her dreams for herself were about to come to fruition through the birth of new hope.

It was a stifling summer in Bombay. Some young children lay sleeping on the sidewalk, sheltering under the large leaves of a rubber tree. People passed by, seemingly oblivious of them. This was Bombay and homeless children were everywhere. They were invisible and they are called the Untouchables.

Nearby, in vacant lots were shanty towns. They were informal settlements characterized by makeshift housing constructed from scraps- metal, wood, leaves, like a bird creating a nest and layering a homestead.

Cows roamed the streets with the cars, against the traffic and everyone just swerved around them. To add to the stench, the sewage system was open- all waste was exposed. It was part of life in the Bombay.

The spillage of homeless flowed into the residential buildings. As the bustling city quieted in the darkest hours of the night, the youth looked for some protection in the hallways of buildings. It was common and accepted. In the mornings, they disappeared into the crowds, engaged in begging, stealing, or menial jobs.

"They are sleeping in the stairwell again. They are so young and have been here for months. Maybe we should help them?" Zina asked Yehuda. They'd found the homeless young men sleeping in their apartment building early that morning.

"I'll go and talk to them."

"What are your names?" Yehuda asked, as he bent down to speak with the young men. They were just waking up and clothed in their *dhoti*–long, rectangular pieces of unstitched cloth wrapped around their waists and were bare-chested. They were startled as Yehuda woke them.

The youth looked at each other, unsure. "I'm Morris, and these are my younger cousins Cornelius and Paul."

Although Morris was the eldest of the brood, he was petite and scrawny. Yet his gentle demeanor was endearing to Yehuda. Cornelius, a bit stockier, had a thick wavy and an unruly head of hair, matching his wild eyes, although he seemed to be a happy young boy. Paul was the pensive one of the bunch.

"Do you work?"

"We all have odd jobs. Cornelius goes to the train station and looks for customers to shine their shoes. Paul goes out looking for food for us, and I look for foreigners in the streets and offer to be their butler."

"*Ha'cha*[1].... Would you like to work for me, Morris? You can be my butler." Looking at Cornelius, Yehuda asked him, "can you clean?"

Cornelius had a wide-open white smile. "*Ha'cha.*" He was beaming.

---

1 *Ha'cha (Hindi)*– okay

"Paul, we will figure out where to place you. You all have a job by me."

Years later, Morris ended up moving to Japan and looking after Yehuda's father, Haim, as his companion. Yehuda strove to live a life of helping others, and this generosity would characterize both Yehuda and Zina as a couple who would become pillars of the Jewish community wherever they lived. Paul would become Yehuda's bookkeeper when the Abrahams moved to New York, and Cornelius was their housekeeper. These men continued to work for the family until their retirement years when they returned to India to be with the families they had grown and supported while living abroad.

Zina wasn't used to someone else taking care of household chores, but she quickly enjoyed being the wife and devoting her attention to her education in Bombay. She got her driver's license, something not a lot of women sought after, which gave her even more freedom. Zina had English lessons, understanding it was a valuable skill. Although she still spoke *Judeo-Farsi* as her home language with Yehuda, as Yehuda did not speak Hebrew well, English remained a secondary official language throughout India.

Zina learned *Mohiniyattam*, a solo Indian dance reliant on the grace and flow of unbroken movement. Although many Indian traditional dances are rhythmic ways of expressing Hindu texts or are acts of religious devotion, Zina learned the dances as cultural rather than religious practices. She fully embraced Indian culture by dressing in saris made of chiffon and raw silk. At one event, she wore an Indian dress with hundreds of coins sewn onto it, along with a silver anklet of bells. She was a walking musical instrument with all that silver jingling.

Bombay was good for Zina, offering her the religious freedom she had grown accustomed to in Israel and the additional freedoms that came with finally having her own household help. Zina's wide taste in cultures available to her in India influenced her daughter's naming. *If I have a girl, I will name her after Shirley Temple,* she thought. She adored watching the young starlet on television. She relished her new adult life and freedoms.

But despite having a full life in Bombay, she missed her family and Israel very much.

Shirley's birth gave Zina the perfect reason to return to Tel Aviv. She had already joined the Women's International Zionist Organization, called WIZO, to remain connected to Israel. WIZO's founders—women and suffragettes married to prominent Zionists in Britain—had begun the organization in 1920. Their work included agriculture, child care, and providing adequate healthcare for pregnant women and infants. WIZO appointed Zina as a leader to take the Jewish women of India on their first trip to Israel. Zina seized the opportunity and left Yehuda in Bombay. She brought Shirley to Israel and placed her with her mother and sisters to look after her while she toured Israel with her Indian friends.

"You always told me that when I got married, I could do anything I wanted," Zina told Dora when she returned.

Dora shifted toddler-sized Shirley from hip to hip while Zina adjusted her bags. "Well, you took it quite literally," she said, sighing. But not so secretly, her daughter's independence and thirst for adventure made her proud.

Zina did not come empty-handed to her sisters. She brought them records of Indian music and showed her sisters how to dance around the house to the flutes and keys of the harmonium. When Shirley cried and fussed over being left behind, they would play

Indian music for her and Yafa took to wearing Zina's clothes and imitating her. It didn't work, but the love was there.

By the time Zina returned to Tel Aviv after a month-long tour, she had discovered that Israel was more than the limited city life she had known. She had a renewed commitment to Jewish philanthropic work that would dominate much of her adult life, enriching the lives she touched.

CHAPTER 15

NEW IN NEW YORK

"What do you think about moving to New York?" Zina asked Yehuda one day. She was nervous but hopeful. Yehuda considered the question, as he often did since India in the 1950s was still undergoing massive shifts as the country settled into independence. Prime Minister Nehru was reorganizing the country's internal states, merging existing states and reorganizing territory along linguistic lines. Bombay became a contested territory. He knew that as Jewish foreigners, he and Zina had no legal protections, nor would they have any say if their neighborhood suddenly came under a different governing body.

"There are many opportunities there; Let's see what we can do," Yehuda agreed, eager as always to explore new avenues.

"America is a free country. We can easily send our children to Jewish schools, and travel anywhere," Zina concluded. "I will contact the Abrams."

Zina had remained in touch with Ethel Abram, the woman who, back in Afghanistan, had treated Zina as her own daughter. Zina had great respect for Ethel as she was an educated woman, working as an Associated Merchandiser for all the major department stores in New York. She was concerned with social justice and was active in her community wherever she lived.

"Ethel, Bombay is not the best place for Shirley to get a Jewish education," Zina said. The remaining Jewish population in India were primarily Indian Jews, many of whom had never been to Israel and did not speak Hebrew.

"We will help you—we can give you guidance," Ethel urged. She and her husband, Lenny, clearly cared for Zina and Yehuda. The family arranged to immigrate to Rego Park in Queens, where the Abrams already lived. Yehuda's mother, Rachel, and his brother Mayer had emigrated first and could attest to the benefits of security and stability being close to Manhattan for business. So, Zina and Yehuda packed their apartment on Queens Road and arrived in Rego Park, New York, immigrants once more.

They were brimming with possibilities. The gem business in India would expand to America as no one from Asia was exporting to America yet. Yehuda and Mayer joined together and opened an office in New York, serving as a satellite office to their growing businesses. In India, Mr. Kanubai, the office manager, would continue to conduct the gem business, primarily emeralds and diamonds, exporting to the newly formed office in New York. Yehuda's youngest brother, Haigul, would eventually move to Milan and open an office to make Italian jewelry with gemstones from Asia. Yehuda's brother-in-law, Avram, married his sister

Tamar and immigrated to Milan, as did his eldest sister Mafrat with her husband, Zakki. Slowly they formed a community there and grew their gem and jewelry business to work in tandem with Yehuda's business. It was a family affair. Family helping family and only in family could you trust.

Rego Park was a predominantly Jewish neighborhood when Zina and Yehuda moved in. It was a neighborhood with a synagogue, Jewish school, kosher butcher, and a direct subway line into Manhattan. Emerging onto the densely populated Queens streets, Zina and Yehuda tilted their heads back, their eyes climbing the enormous buildings. Streams of buses and yellow cabs honked, belching gray smoke. Pedestrians rushed by like wind-up dolls, colliding and barely taking notice.

Away from the bustle was their first home on Wetherole Street. A red brick three story row house shared with Zina, Yehuda, Shirley, and Rachel on the first floor. Mayer and his family lived on the second floor, and the third floor was reserved for guests.

By the 1960s, Afghan Jews began immigrating *en masse*, taking advantage of the laws allowing them to immigrate and maintain their Afghani citizenship. As more Bukharan and Afghan Jews immigrated to the United States, the third floor of the Abraham home became a refuge for them in the early stages of starting a new life. Their home became a revolving door of tears, laughter, friendship, noise, and loud Shabbat celebrations. These guests were friends or distant relatives, sometimes friends of friends. The relations didn't matter: there was a place in Rego Park that would welcome these families and help them build a life.

Through Zina's work as a hostess, under the direction of her mother-in-law Rachel, there was a joyful Jewish community and a kosher home. On Friday nights, the dining room swelled with merchants, jewelers, and immigrants, ensuring that their shared home became a pillar for the Afghan and Bukharan immigrant communities. Their home always had a distinctive smell of rice, cardamom, and chicken, as juices thickened in their pots, rice hardened into a delectable crust, and steamy aromas escaped from under their lids, permeating waves into every room. Ethel and Lenny continued to be included in all their holiday celebrations. They were happy to be adopted by this lively, rich family and culture.

Shirley gleefully played with cousins that had temporarily moved from Italy to New York. Sadly, Yehuda's sister Tamar, who had been formerly living in Milan, gave birth to a son that died at childbirth due to the inadequate medical attention she received from her doctor. The labor was going fine until the doctor intervened and forcibly shoved the infant back into her uterus. Tamar and Avram believed that this was an anti-Semitic attack. For this reason, when Tamar was subsequently pregnant, the Lazarov's moved to New York to birth with better medical care.

At the interim, Shirley and her Italian cousins played American-style games such as "Cowboys and Indians" in the garden, shrieking with delight while the ladies enjoyed sipping their *choi* and sucking on rock candy. The Lazarovs incorporated bits and pieces of American culture into their new Jewish-American identities. Other than Shabbat, when shopping was prohibited, the family, including their Italian cousins and aunts, would walk most days down the block to Alexander's department store.

The Rego Park location of Alexander's Department store had just opened in 1959 on Queens Boulevard and 63rd Drive.

Alexander's was *the* place to shop, as customers came for the clothes and stayed for lunch at the onsite lunch counters. For the youngest children, Alexander's was a massive playground. There was no better place to hide than behind the racks of skirts and no better place to become lost.

However, Zina and her sisters were not as interested in shopping or dining. While other customers pulled blouses and skirts off the racks and into their carts to purchase, they pulled blouses and skirts close to examine the seams, the stitching, and the folds of fabric.

Why purchase these items when they could recreate them with their sewing experience? Zina mused, smiling conspiratorially. They would finger the various fabrics on display and head home with new fashion ideas swimming in their heads.

Zina loved fashion and enjoyed designing, and sewing up her creativity into works of art. She made monthly trips to the local smoke shop near the 71st Continental Avenue subway station to purchase the latest *Vogue*. She could barely read or write, but she loved looking at showy high-end clothing and fantasizing about whose next wedding she could wear her home sewn evening gown that looked like it was plucked off the runway. In one instance she designed a charmeuse silk dress in daring colors of purple and fuchsia with puffed shoulders resembling flowers. Her flamboyant style of dress was a stark contrast to the chador uniform she was confined to back in Afghanistan. Perhaps this was her rebellion, and yet it was also a way to maintain her status as Queen Bee amongst her sisters and peers. Years later she encouraged her daughters to wear the latest fashion trends, allowing them to dress as they wished. Through them she gave herself the adolescent freedom that she never had.

To further advance her designing skills, she enrolled in Parson's School of Design night classes where she'd learn to draw her design whims. From there she'd create a muslin and play around with different fabrics to see which one would fall better. In her spare time, she was engaged with her helper- the Singer sewing machine, as her aid.

Further down the road on 108th Street was where they bought their produce. Cruising wide aisles, in awe of the assortment of food, Zina suddenly saw piles of honeydews among other fruits. She was the keenest shopper in all of Queens. She investigated by smelling, squeezing, and shaking the watermelons, pineapples, and pomegranates. She did everything short of biting before making her pick and occasionally plucked a grape off the vine to taste if it was worthwhile. Thereafter came the bargaining with the shop owner with steely confidence, in a country that didn't bargain! "Mam, this is the price. It's a fixed price." She was unaccustomed to this way, as everywhere she'd resided thus far was a culture of haggling.

After Zina had returned home and prepared the produce for her lunch each day, she fell onto the living room sofa and planted herself in front of the television anticipating another drama from her favorite soap opera, *As the World Turns*. With one eye fixed on her salad and the other fastened to the TV, Zina was learning English. This snapshot captured an ever present split in Zina. Although thoroughly a Bukharan Jew, haggling over the price of produce, she was also embracing life in America by always trying to advance her education.

CHAPTER 16

FROM PINK TO WHITE AND BEYOND

Yehuda continued to manage the gem business and found more business opportunities including exporting bails of clothing and General Motor tires to Afghanistan, which was extremely lucrative. Having come from a long line of Silk Road merchants, traders, and shepherds, Yehuda drew from his mercantile past. No one in America knew or thought to open an economic vessel to Afghanistan; they had barely heard of Afghanistan.

With more economic growth, he purchased the family's first single-family home in New York: a house on Booth Street-a pink house still in Rego Park.

Thereafter, Yehuda helped to purchase a home for Zina's parents and her unmarried siblings on Wetherole Street around the corner from them. Family ties and living close to one's family remained the cultural dictum.

The Abrahams lived next door to the Lupinos, who had no children. Similar to how Ethel and Lenny treated Zina as their daughter in Afghanistan, the Italian family cared deeply about Shirley and the addition of a new brother, Gideon. The neighbors' kindness was all the more important to Shirley's childhood because these were some of the first Americans with whom the Abraham family became close.

The Italians next door always greeted Shirley warmly with cookies and opened the door for her to see more of American life. This contrasted with their neighbors around the corner on Wetherole Street, who were a Catholic family and clearly hated Jews, ordering their family collie dog to attack and chase Shirley along with her Aunt Bracha. That was their first memorable brush with antisemitism.

The second house, the White House, became a central hub for the Abrahams. Yehuda and Mayer purchased the home for their mother, Rachel. Their father moved to Tokyo, where he opened an office exporting pearls as part of the growing family business with his sons.

Showing great respect, every day before he and Mayer went to work, they stopped by the White House to visit their mother and drink *choi*. In the afternoon, when they left work, the sons returned to the White House before returning to their wives and children for another cup of *choi* and perhaps a meal. The sons remained devoted to their mother for the entirety of her life. Rachel kept the White House and tended a vineyard in the backyard, along the chain link fence, following the tradition in her family started by her father, who had become wealthy through growing grapes and exporting wine. Rachel regularly made wine and jam for her family and stored it in her cellar.

Family was everything to Zina. Despite all the upheavals of immigration, all eight of her siblings lived within five blocks of each other. The White House was a much grander home than 63rd Drive and soon became what 63rd Drive had been: a staple in the Afghani and Bukharan community for friends and relatives and friends of friends. It was a free place to live for anyone within the circle of family and friends until they could get on their feet and move out.

"Thank G-d, the gem business is providing well for our family." Zina turned to Yehuda over breakfast one morning as he tapped the back of his spoon to break open a hard-boiled egg. "You are very good to my sisters and their husbands, helping them enter the family business right away, giving them some security."

While not likely to fan himself with compliments, Yehuda confirmed, "I do not view anyone in my business as competition; there is room for everyone." Yehuda was not legal minded nor strategic. He had never insisted on contracts and hadn't even known to do so. Yehuda came from a corner of the world where a handshake was all you needed. In Central Asia, merchants formed trusted relationships that lasted lifetimes, and passed them on to their children and grandchildren, with only a verbal agreement. A man's word was his honor, his face and reputation, his contract and currency. Who would think a man would want to tarnish his own name and jeopardize trust? Yehuda never felt ill-will toward anyone that he employed, many of whom eventually ventured out on their own to become his competition.

Yehuda advanced his kindness to his extended family, as he knew they also had to make a living.

In keeping with the family's value to maintain close proximity to each other, and as a result of the family's financial success, Yehuda and Zina were able to purchase a grand house on the same street as the White House, just two blocks down the road. This was a monumental turning point in Zina's life. They could afford a live-in housekeeper, which would enable Zina to continue to help her mother-in-law Rachel with the daily chores of running a household including doctor visits, shopping, cooking, and hosting a stream of guests. She finally felt free, and the master of her own domain.

This coincided with the birth of their third child, Jackie, who was a healthy chubby nine-month-old when they moved into this house. In the 1960s it was considered passé to breastfeed. Her American obstetrician, Dr. Immerman, told her that it was crude to stick one's nipple into an infant's mouth. It was primitive and unsanitary. She was told bottle feeding was the healthiest and most enlightened way to mother one's child. She did not want to appear Third World and desperately wanted to catch up to modernity, and in all frankness, not be tied down, so she happily complied.

Jackie was born at a time when Zina felt most settled. Their new home included many fun and personal details: a hidden bar within the library of the living room, a diorama of a boat built into the wall unit, butler buttons with an indicator panel in the kitchen, a maid's quarters, and a finished wood paneled basement with a wet bar where many parties were enjoyed. This was a far cry from their modest beginnings. They maintained this home as a thriving cultural center for their community, as well as a warm landing pad for new immigrants. Their prosperity was not an end unto itself; it afforded them an opportunity to be of service and remained open to anyone who needed a place to launch a transition to life in a country where they could enjoy religious and financial freedom.

When it came time to decide on education, Zina asked her Jewish neighbor with school-aged children where she should send her children. "To yeshiva," the woman suggested, "Yeshiva Dov Revel."

Yeshiva Dov Revel taught children from nursery to eighth grade, and all of Zina's children would attend—albeit with mixed experiences. Just as Dora had unevenly divided herself amongst her children, Zina had done the same. Each morning she woke up her boys, because apparently the alarm clock was not loud enough to wake them up. She prepared them a proper cooked breakfast and drove them to school. Every single day. Always tardy. Shirley who was a much more conscientious and studious girl did not want to rely on the free drive, otherwise she would have been perpetually late. Instead, Shirley arose from sleep on her own, made breakfast and took the yellow school bus at the corner.

The girls, however, were privileged in another way, a way that satisfied Zina's yearning to be formally educated with cultural and artistic inclusion from which she was deprived. Shirley and Dahlia, born in 1969, eight years after Jackie, both had private piano lessons with a strict piano teacher, who would use his pointer regularly to snap at the keys if they played a tune incorrectly. He demanded that they follow his instructions to the note and not deviate, which made the lessons feel like punishment rather than fun.

While Zina beamed that her daughters were learning *do-reh-mi-fah-so-lah-ti-do*, the girls didn't appreciate the strictness from the teacher. Dora, of course, was so proud that her granddaughters followed in the footsteps of her pristine education.

Dahlia was creative just like her mother. She would often play by herself. For example she'd build a dollhouse from a cardboard box, and make paper dolls for her little abode. Recognizing her creativity, which came more from a lack of anything to play with, Zina enrolled Dahlia with a private painting teacher when she was twelve years old. *Maybe Dahlia can draw the designs for the dresses I'd like to sew,* Zina secretly thought to herself.

Russia was considered the capital for ballet, and in honor of her mother's Russian roots, Zina enrolled Shirley and Dahlia in after-school ballet classes. As this was Zina's fantasy for her daughters and not necessarily her daughters' desire, both piano lessons and ballet lessons never amounted to anything.

At Dov Revel, the curriculum was taught to the children in both Hebrew and English, following Rabbi Revel's design in an attempt to maintain Jewish cultural life in the secular world. The *yeshiva* ultimately accomplished what Zina and Yehuda desired for their children: to grow up with a particular Jewish education that taught Hebrew and fostered a connection to Israel. This was one of their ways of ensuring Jewish continuity.

The education, however, was not always what Zina's children wanted. The yeshiva was primarily Ashkenazi in its student population, and many teachers were Shoah survivors. The Abraham children were some of the few Mizrachi Jews in the school. Shirley felt disconnected because she and her siblings had not been exposed to Ashkenazi traditions, and the Ashkenazi institution and students were not interested in learning about, or acknowledging, the rich Jewish history of the Central Asian tradition. The children saw and felt that the school's administration treated them poorly, believing that Mizrachi students were inferior in class.

In school, the siblings were placed in the lowest level C classes: classes reserved for ESL learners, immigrant children, and anyone considered too slow for the more advanced classrooms. Dahlia, felt especially ostracized. Although born in America, Dahlia was viewed as other worldly and undesirable, because of her darker complexion and her family heralding from a foreign country no one had heard of at the time. She was not quite white in Ashkenazi eyes. Fellow Jews treated her like a counterfeit. Nevertheless, she soon developed a special bond with her nursery teacher, Rise, who would look after her while her mother traveled abroad.

Despite her children's mixed experiences at Yeshiva, as more and more Bukharan, Afghan, and Iranian Jews immigrated to New York with their young children, parents turned to Zina. Where do *your* children go to school? Following Zina's recommendation, they, too, enrolled their children in Yeshiva Dov Revel. Zina was always proud of building a community with strong Jewish roots where children all learned to speak Hebrew fluently.

CHAPTER 17

ISRAEL–A HOME AWAY FROM HOME

Trips to Israel were treasured as a home away from home, not just a vacation. When Zina and her family visited Israel for the summers, the family lived in one of the apartments that Haim, Yehuda's father, had built back when the State of Israel was first declared independent. Likewise, Hasid shared the same ideology that Israel is our Jewish homeland, so he, too, invested and bought land that the family could always have as a safe haven. He purchased two parcels of land in Tel Aviv for the family: both agricultural parcels, one in Ramat Hasharon and the other in Holon.

In the summer, Zina and Yehuda sent their children for a month to sleep away camps in Israel, furthering their Hebrew language skills, personal ties to Jewish tradition, and the connection to Israel. After camp, the rest of their time was in their family apartment- as natives. Neighbors would knock on the door and invite them to come to play with them—games of *machanayim*, an Israeli version of dodgeball, in the streets and Chinese jump rope called *goomi* that merged hopscotch with elements of cat's cradle. "Shirli, Shirli, come play!" was heard daily as the Abraham children were seamlessly welcomed into the social fabric by the local Israeli children.

However, in the summer of 1963, Zina and Yehuda took their most significant trip to Israel, with Shirley and Gideon. It was a momentous year for the family as there were three special occasions taking place. Zina's younger sister Tamar, married Yehuda's younger brother, Haigul. Mayer's daughter, Rosa also got married a week from that wedding.

The last celebration was for Zina and Yehuda's grandparents, Agajan and Chana, who were turning one hundred years old. And their children had a special gift in mind: a dedication of a Sefer Torah in their grandparents' honor. This was particularly poignant because Agajan's father had been a *Shamash* in Afghanistan. This would be a gift and an honor to his great work in perpetuity. Mayer, who still made frequent trips to Afghanistan, brought the Sefer Torahs to Israel— an ode to their heritage.

The dedication party took place in Tel Aviv and was distinctly Bukharan with traditional *doira* drums beat throughout the event. Agajan and Chana presided, resplendent in head-coverings, silk, and gold-threaded flowing gowns in brilliant colors. Each grandchild humbly approached the sweet, mild-mannered, white-bearded *Bobo* and asked for a blessing. He placed his hands on their heads and blessed them. They in turn kissed his hand as a sign of respect and love.

These Sefer Torahs ultimately became a gift to Jewish communities across Israel, as they would travel from synagogue to synagogue.

CHAPTER 18

CLOSURE FOR DORA

Dora enjoyed her home in New York, but continued to miss her own family still in the Uzbek Soviet Socialist Republic. From the time she got married, she had not seen her family. The political climate in Soviet Uzbek continued to be precarious. Both Jews and Muslims faced religious repression and a "Russification" of the state that would last for decades.

It would take thirty years until Dora at the age of fifty-five could see her family again, as, even once she'd obtained United States citizenship, travel restrictions continued to the Soviet Union and Soviet states. But in Spring of 1966, she booked a flight back to Tashkent, in Soviet Uzbek, to reunite with her mother Bracha, her brothers Avram and Isaac, and sisters Freda, Miriam, and Malka.

Throughout Dora's vast time apart from her family, she feverishly posted letters to them with photos of her children chronicling details of their life. Although oceans apart, when they finally did reunite, the shared stories continued as if they had always been by each other's side.

While most of the immediate family lived in Tashkent, her sister Freda was living in the Turkmen Soviet Socialist Republic and excitedly traveled to Tashkent to see her sister. They'd left each other as young adults and now reunited with families of their own.

Dora was elated to spend three weeks at her sister Miriam's home. Miriam was quite an industrious woman who'd designed and built her palatial home with a large open terrace from the ground up. Many of the homes built in Tashkent did not consider the Bukharan's family structure, which tended towards bigger and extended families. In Miriam's home lived her mother, Bracha, who was 85 years old and suffered from sclerosis. It was common for multi generations to live together and take care of each other.

The Soviet architects used a common standard for housing in the entire Union. And it is also telling that most of the plans were drawn by Moscow-based architects who rarely or never visited Tashkent and their big families. 'Cities were not supposed to suit the customs of the inhabitants; inhabitants were supposed to transform their customs to suit the new Soviet city' (Stronski, 2011). It was for this reason that Miriam designed and constructed her home to suit the family's needs.

She hosted her sister Dora in her home every day, and would have preferred for her to stay with them, but Soviet Uzbek did not allow family members visiting from abroad to stay with family. Dora stayed at the luxurious Hotel Uzbekistan located in the center of town.

The hotel had an imposing brutal exterior style that was an extension of Socialist ideology: strong and imposing, and expected to last forever like the state. Socialism was hardwearing, robust, and available to all people- like the raw concrete to build this hotel. It was all show-an aggressive exterior, while the rooms were quite bland and basic, representing the uniformity and simplicity of socialism.

As a child growing up in Soviet Uzbek, Dora used to watch camel caravans, as well as herds of sheep amble along rough stone paved streets. She never envisioned that one day she would be back in her homeland and the camels would be replaced by taxis. Every day she hailed a taxi to her sister, Miriam, and spent the entire day enveloped in her family.

She missed Russia and her family so much and wished that they could all live together as they once had long ago. She dreamed for years to be close to them, to see them again, and she repeatedly said to her family, "My dreams have come true."

The only strain on her heart was the whereabouts of her long-lost cousin Manny. Her mother's nephew who had left Russia in the early 1920's was still missing.

Zina was inspired to travel to Russia thereafter and meet her extended family. She would return to the country that imprisoned her thirty-eight years ago.

In 1971, Zina, Yehuda, their son Gideon, and her sister Rosa made the trip to Tashkent. Filled with relief and gratitude, Zina met her grandmother, aunts and uncles, and many cousins, including her first cousin Liza—who was living with and taking care of Zina's grandmother. Zina asked why Liza had not moved to Israel, especially as the Soviet Union was allowing repatriation for Bukharan Jews. But Liza was afraid to leave her extended family behind, and by the time she considered the move, the quota for Jews to leave had closed.

Liza's *only* option was the hope that if she took her Aunt Bracha with her, their applications would still be considered, as she'd be traveling with an elderly woman in her eighties. As always, Zina promised that she and her family would do anything to help. Thanks to Yehuda and Zina's financial contribution, the family were able to immigrate in the year 1974, and Bracha spent the end of her life in Israel in the care of her niece in Netanya.

When Bracha passed away, it was with incredible luck that Zina found space in a crowded burial plot in Jerusalem, *Har Menuchot*. Even more incredible, Zina ensured Bracha would be buried near the rest of her family. And then, when Dora later passed away in 1993, Zina ensured she was buried close to her mother, as they had spent so many decades apart and now were reunited in Jerusalem. To this day, Israel remains integral to all generations of the family.

CHAPTER 19

FINDING LONG LOST FAMILY

"I have long-lost family in Colombia," Zina mentioned casually to her dinner guests with her mother Dora by her side. She set down a huge platter of Bukharan *pilau* bejeweled in slivered carrots and raisins and began to serve their Columbian guest, who was Yehuda's business associate.

The man perked up, raising an eyebrow. "Oh?"

Zina was well-known for her warmth and hospitality, for her plates of delicious food, and for her ability to entertain guests. But she veered away from the usual small talk and took a shot in the dark: "I have a cousin who left Israel for Colombia decades ago. His father—my grandmother's brother—never saw him again," Zina explained to her visitor. A tinge of sadness colored her voice. "My mother always spoke of this long-lost nephew of hers."

"What is his name?" the visitor asked, setting down his red wine resolutely.

"Manny Mosheyov..." Dora perked up and replied with tempered curiosity.

"I think I know of him! I'm going to try to find him for you." Dora and Zina gasped. *Could this be possible?*

Amazed at how small the world *might* be, both women still kept their expectations low. But searching for a Bukharan Jew named Manny in a country with very few Jews was easier than expected. They never imagined such a fortuitous connection. Once Manny was found, Zina extended an invitation immediately. In less than two years, Manny would travel to New York and reconnect with the family.

"Bring him some paper— quick!" Zina's three children rushed to get their markers and paper and brought them to the dining table where Manny and Dora were sitting. They had no way of communicating with Manny, as he did not speak English, Bukharan, or Russian; apparently, he had forgotten these languages but was not short on gestures, photos from Colombia and Spanish.

"Go ahead, tell us the story as best you can," Shirley encouraged Manny, sliding the paper in front of him. As always, Zina didn't hesitate to embrace her family. Their dining table had been the central gathering force to so many interesting visitors and their tales, but this was a fascinating journey to try and unwind for the family—language barriers and all.

Manny shared photos of his family, pointing to a photo of him with his parents, expressing how they had had moved to Jerusalem in 1923. He wrote the number "12" to indicate that he was only twelve years old when his family left Soviet Uzbek. With few English words and through painful, laugh-out-loud miming, alongside drawings on the paper, and photos he portrayed the events of his life. They learned that although Jerusalem was—and *is*—a dream for many Jewish families, Manny wasn't happy there. In words and images, he explained:

"Around my eighteenth birthday, I ran away to the port in Haifa, then onto a ship to Santa Marta, and a new life in a Colombian city on the northern shore. Due to the industrial boom in the 1930s, I would make a living first selling fabric and textiles, then selling shoes, before finally settling in the pawn industry of jewelry resale." The children listened, interpreted, and pulled together his story with awe and fascination. "The 1940s and 1950s were difficult decades for Colombia," Manny continued. "It was a period known as *La Violencia*. Due to internal political strife between the Liberal and Conservative parties, an estimated 200,000 people were killed in the decade between 1948 and 1958."

"How was it for you, as a Jew in Colombia?" Dora asked although everyone knew the familiar story of antisemitism all too well.

"Colombia is a very Catholic country. To practice Judaism," Manny shared with the family in a serious tone, "I held secret meetings with other Jewish friends. It was taboo to speak openly about being Jewish. Neighbors questioned me for not attending church, and I always had to come up with an excuse."

After dinner, Manny turned to Zina as she showed him to his guest room. "You know, I am married to a Colombian, a non-Jewish woman. . . but I put on a *kippah* on Yom Kippur. It is such a welcome difference to be in New York with you all in a free country."

Manny reveled in the religious freedom and the Jewish community New York had to offer. His soul longed for this connection.

It would be six months before he would return to his pregnant wife in Colombia.

Manny had been so affected by his time in New York. He was surrounded by his long lost family: so many generations, holding *many* memories that he had missed. He was holding his newborn girl in his arms and it was for this reason that he named her Zina, after his cousin in New York.

Upon his return to Colombia, Manny began to share his childhood in Israel, his Jewish lineage, and his hopes for a Jewish future with his wife. After a taste of religious freedom, he returned to Colombia with a plan- work and save money and move to New York so that his family could grow up with a Jewish heritage.

The years went by, and more children arrived. *"Estudiar Ingles[1],"* he told his wife and daughters. Manny gathered his family to share plans he had been working on since traveling home from the United States.

The family chimed in to share what little English they knew— "dog," "television," and "Coca-Cola,"—smiling and promising that they would keep learning the language.

"This is my dream for us. To get away from the turmoil out there." Manny looked out the window and coughed again, the rough, throaty sounds mirroring his underlying concern for the political situation in Colombia. It continued to be unstable in urban and rural areas as the government-backed army attacked villages to root out communists and bandits. What the family didn't know was Manny was growing sick with lung cancer. Before he could fulfill his dream of bringing his family to America, he passed away.

---

1 *Estudiar Ingles (Spanish)-* study english

"Zina, Manny Mosheyov's granddaughter called Yehuda's office looking for him. Since you both were away, Aldythe gave her my number," Rosa informed Zina one day.

Zina smiled, recollecting her long-lost family and how the bonds endured now, all these years later. Manny's daughter Zina had stayed in contact with them through letters, but sometime after he passed away, they'd lost touch. *I wander what she wants?* Zina thought.

Through a translator, Manny's granddaughter Davina conveyed to Zina that Colombia had become too dangerous and too difficult to make a living. She just graduated college as a computer engineer and could not find work in Colombia. Her visa application to New York had been denied. Davina had found her grandfather's correspondence with Yehuda's company letterhead and had decided to contact her American family. She hoped Zina would help her, as her dream was like her grandfather's—to leave Colombia.

Zina told Davina to reach out to an immigration lawyer and inform him she has family in America. Zina assured her that she would provide whatever she needed to get out of Colombia.

Davina was grateful to have support and followed up soon after that, informing Zina that the attorney said there was "No way out of Colombia on a visa."

Zina was quick to reply for Davina to go to a Rabbi and tell him that her grandfather was Jewish. There is the Law of Return to Israel. It says that a person can come to Israel and become an Israeli citizen if that person has at least one Jewish grandparent or is married to a Jewish person.

Davina would be allowed Israeli citizenship. The only issue was that she would first need to prove that her grandfather was Jewish and obtain Jewish Certification. This would be particularly hard as Davina had not grown up Jewish, neither had her mother, and there were no local synagogues to seek further guidance on this matter.

Nonetheless with Davina being resourceful as she was, she found a Rabbi on a list approved by the Israeli Chief Rabbinate. This rabbi would then have to present documents: a letter of recommendation and any documentation that her grandfather was Jewish. Zina and Yehuda of course obliged to help in the process.

The Consulate in Colombia sent Davina to the Grand Rabbi of Bogota, who asked if Davina knew anyone who had known her grandfather and could testify that he was Jewish. Yehuda had business contacts in Colombia since he imported emeralds from there, and one of his associates facilitated in presenting evidence that Manny was Jewish to the Grand Rabbi of Bogota.

In July of 2001, Davina left Colombia to make *aliyah*, (immigrate) to Israel. The following year, her mother, father, sister, and brother followed, making them the first family from Manny's line to return to Israel. The news of the life they had made spread to the rest of the family, and soon, all six of Manny's children and their families immigrated as well. There was some family strife, as Manny had another Colombian family from another woman before Davina's grandmother. The families were embittered over this. Nonetheless, when the second wife of Manny found out that her ex's family had moved to Israel, they all employed the same strategy and also made aliyah.

The irony was not lost on the family: Manny fled Israel as a young man, only to have generations of his offspring return, embracing Judaism and their heritage. Israel was the family's history and future. And this immigration would not have been possible without the group's efforts, their commitment, and his desire for the entire family to have religious freedom and a connection to Israel.

CHAPTER 20

DIASPORA IN ASIA

Zina and Yehuda were overlooking the makeshift synagogue they had created on the fourth floor of their building. In the late 1960s Yehuda and Mayer purchased a five-story building in the Maheasak business center of Bangkok and hired a Thai office manager, Howard, to communicate with the locals. They were brokers to the miners throughout the entire colored-stone gem industry. Customers could select gems at the best possible price, while Yehuda and their company, Afasia, would broker the deals, negotiating for fairness and ethical practices.

Not many foreigners traveled to Asia. Thailand was undeveloped, lacking western infrastructure and relying on dirt roads. Still, what might have been a hindrance to some travelers was an advantage to Yehuda's gem business. With no one traveling to these distant places, Afasia captured the entire gem industry at the time. Albeit the goal was to ensure everyone was happy and could make a living.

Zina thought back to how she and Yehuda, along with Mayer and some other members of the Afghan Jewish community, started the Sephardic Jewish Congregation of Queens, an orthodox synagogue, in the 1970s, and how they got that off the ground. Zina remembered the synagogue's Purim parties, Hanukkah gatherings, and luncheons—many of which she had hosted. Zina missed her social life. She thought back to her work at the sisterhood, hosting fundraising luncheons, going to different stores, and asking for donations. The money would then go back to the synagogue to provide for Jewish community life.

She looked around and wondered, *what are the needs here*? Yehuda chimed in as if he read her mind, "You make contributions to the community, Zina, wherever you go. I need your help here. I want you by my side. You can teach the cooks, Sumsi and Mali, our Bukharan dishes for our guests and customers coming from abroad."

Zina heard her mother's voice in her head, "*Never leave your husband. Go wherever he goes.*" She recalled how her mother was separated many years from her father due to his business travels. Zina chose to be by Yehuda's side, away from her children once Dahlia reached ten years old. Zina felt more freedom to leave for a couple months at a time, leaving the children with the live-in help and surrounding family to drop in and check on them once in a while. *I am needed here. This Jewish mission is larger than Yehuda and me, and I am willing to leave New York to build a Jewish life here. Otherwise, there is almost nothing Jewish here without us.* Zina showed the cooks how to prepare kosher food and convert all her Bukharan dishes to vegetarian ones. Zina's cooking style was inspired by every culture she encountered, which made it both unusual and delightful. She instinctively knew how to integrate her native Bukharan cooking into any new cuisine she was immersed in.

When Yehuda and Mayer set up an office in Thailand, there were many challenges for them, as there were only a few Jews in the country at the time. There was no synagogue and nowhere to purchase kosher meat. It took years before more Jews in the gem business traveled to Thailand and did business directly with Afasia. As more Jews traveled to Bangkok, Yehuda turned his living quarters on the fourth floor into a synagogue. With ten men, they formed a *minyan*[1], wrapped their tefillin, and prayed.

Decades passed before they could get a rabbi to fly in to kosher some chickens for consumption. "Zina, the rabbi from Hong Kong will be here soon."

"Really? Why?"

"He is flying into *shecht*[2] chickens for the community."

"Oh great. We will have chicken for Shabbat." On Friday nights, Zina and Yehuda hosted free Shabbat dinners, filling their tables with Jews searching to connect while abroad. Weekly, they hosted up to fifty people at a time.

Men and women exiting the Israeli Defense Forces, the IDF, traveled East as a break from the rigidness of the army. Traveling throughout Southeast Asia became a rite of passage for many IDF soldiers. They congregated along Khao San Road, a hub for backpackers due to cheap guest houses. Immense food stalls filled the roads, permeating pungent smells of rats, chicken, and catfish.

---

1 *Minyan (Hebrew)*– a quorum of ten Jewish men
2 *Shecht (Hebrew)*– kosher slaughter

These travelers found the Abraham family after Yehuda began advertising free Shabbat dinners in an Israeli newspaper. Yehuda was soon listed as the contact person in the *World Jewish Guidebook for Travelers*. He and Zina were proud of bringing these travelers into their homes for Shabbat dinner and having Jewish company.

"Eventually, the Jewish community of Thailand may grow large enough that holding a *minyan* in the office will be no longer suitable," Yehuda mused. "One day, we may need to find a bigger place." Zina smiled, believing in their shared outlook and work, even across the globe.

And one day, they did. The Abraham family, along with some other members of the community, rented a space for a synagogue, *Even Chen*—meaning "warm stone." The growing Jewish community was partly due to Yehuda and Mayer hiring Israeli men to work in their office. Israeli, because they were the only ones adventurous enough to live in Asia. When these bachelors were inclined to marry, they left Bangkok, returned to Israel to find a spouse, and then settled back in Bangkok as husband and wife, further growing the Jewish community. However, even with the new synagogue, there was still not a stable Jewish presence in this young community.

"We're finally here!" Zina, Yehuda and Mayer had waited in a long line for hours to seek guidance from *the Rebbe*, Menachem Mendel Schneerson, A Russian-Jewish immigrant and leader of Chabad-Lubavitch—an Orthodox Hasidic movement. He'd taken up the mantle of Chabad leadership in 1951 when his father-in-law passed away, and from then on, he worked to reinvigorate and expand Chabad. To the Rebbe, this mission meant placing Jewish centers and outreach everywhere. It meant that no matter where a Jewish person lived, they would not be isolated or cut off from Judaism.

On Sundays, the Rebbe held open houses at his home on 770 Eastern Parkway in Brooklyn, where visitors would come to him with problems and blessings. Here he would offer them advice and a blessing, along with a dollar as a metaphorical exchange that signaled the giving of charity.

Rabbi Hecht, their rabbi from the Sephardic Congregation of Queens, invited the Abrahams to visit the Rebbe. Yehuda stepped up, bowed his head, then looked up into the eyes the Rebbe, and informed him: "We also live in Bangkok, Thailand."

He gave them a blessing and a dollar. Yehuda and Zina made their way out, inch by inch, through the packed corridor. Nearing the exit, a member from the inner circle of the Rebbe caught up with Zina and Yehuda and asked them to return to the Rebbe.

"Do you have a *mikvah*[3] in Bangkok?" asked the Rebbe.

"No, we don't," they replied in tandem. There was no mikvah, a ritual family bath important to maintain family purity laws, at the time, and without a place for Jews to obtain ritual purity post-menstruation, childbirth, and pre-burial, there would be no stable Orthodox Jewish presence.

"Without a *mikvah*, you cannot build and sustain a Jewish community." He handed the Abrahams *five* dollars and said, "Build a *mikvah*. Here's your first donation."

The Rebbe made sure to keep in touch with them and sent them an encouraging letter:

---

3 *Mikvah (Hebrew)*– spiritual immersion in a natural spring of water

Dear Mayer and Yehuda,

There is surely no need to emphasize to you at length the great importance of a Mikvah, which is one of the essential, divinely given mitzvot, which has an impact on not only the persons observing it but also on their children and their children's children to the end of posterity. It is also a mitzvah that hastens the Geula Shleima, meaning complete redemption, which is connected with purity, as it is written, "I shall sprinkle upon you, pure water and you shall be pure."(Ezek: 36:25)

The Bangkok community was small. Perhaps two or three women would ever use the mikvah, yet the Rebbe felt it was essential to build one, even for so few. The Abrahams was always open to new challenges and passionate about Jewish causes, sharing the Rebbe's enthusiasm for the cause.

One year, in the late 1970s, the Abrahams and members of the Afghan Jewish community brought the Rebbe as a birthday gift, precious historical documents. When Mayer made a toast, the Rebbe told him the best birthday gift would be the Mikvah in Bangkok.

A rabbi needed to be called in to determine the right spot in Bangkok to begin construction. Bangkok, sometimes called the Venice of the East, is built above canals, which makes digging deep into the ground difficult. The Mikvah would need a unique design, with the pool above ground. The challenge was finding a water source from a natural spring that would flow directly into the *mikvah* without being pumped by technology.

With each new proposed construction site, something was wrong until finally, everything was right. Despite the many challenges involved, the Rebbe never gave up. Every time the Abrahams visited the Rebbe, he would ask them: "What is with the mikvah in Bangkok?"

It took over ten years of gathering permits and donations before the *mikvah* was constructed. They dedicated the first *mikvah* in Thailand to Yehuda's departed mother, and named it, *Mikvah Rachel.*

Once the *mikvah* was built, a rabbi finally agreed to live in Thailand. Only then did the Rebbe sent Chabad families to Thailand. And they served the growing Jewish community with religious guidance, humanitarian aid, kosher food, and social services.

The legacy of the Rebbe, who passed away in 1996, remained in Thailand and was entangled with the legacy the Abrahams started, as the Chabad of Thailand used its resources to eventually build *Ohr Menachem,* a massive community hall, synagogue, and kosher restaurant off the main traveler's road of Khao San.

On one of Zina and Yehuda's trips to Israel in about 2010, Zina sought out the Torah scrolls that were gifted to their grandparents for their one-hundredth birthday. The scrolls had been traveling through Israel for years and years.

As more and more of the Abraham family left Israel for America or to join Yehuda's gem business in growing satellite offices in Asia and Europe, there were not a lot of families left to keep track of them, until they finally got lost.

Zina wanted the Torahs to be in the very synagogue Yehuda started, *Even Chen.*

The last time they had seen the Torah scrolls had been maybe in the late seventies. Zina had set about tracking down the scrolls, spending her time making phone calls that continuously yielded no results or conflicting results. She returned to Israel and continued her inquiries but found that each person she asked gave her a different answer: "It was *this* synagogue." or "No, it was "*that* synagogue." She kept calling and calling until finally, she found one of the scrolls and then, eventually, the other. After two decades, and many round of phone calls and false starts, she found them again.

Zina took a taxi to the synagogue and was shown where the Torah was kept. However, this Torah was the larger of the two: too heavy to carry, and she had come alone, because, Yehuda had recently been diagnosed with multiple myeloma, and heavy lifting was no longer an option.

While she tried to plan how to move the Torah, the taxi driver calmly walked into the synagogue, lifted the Torah scroll, and carried it to the car. When the taxi dropped her off at her sister-in-law's apartment—where they would keep the Torah until further decisions were made—the driver, without hesitation, carried the Torah up the flights of stairs and into the living room.

One of the Torah scrolls was no longer kosher: the words were beginning to fade, and the scroll was, in its current state, unusable. So, Zina sent it to a *Sofer*[4] for repairs.

The repaired scroll would go to *Even Chen* in Bangkok and the other to Chabad in Hong Kong. Zina felt "repaired," too. Fulfillment and satisfaction with her accomplishments washed over her.

On August 6, 2016, a *Sefer Torah* party was dedicated by Zina and Yehuda's son Gideon, in memory of Yehuda, upon his passing in 2014 at the very synagogue he started with his brother Mayer in Bangkok. And Zipor and Shimon's daughter, Hanna, who lives in Hong Kong, dedicated the second Torah to her synagogue in memory of her father, who had lived in Hong Kong after he left Afghanistan.

---

4 *Sofer (Hebrew)*– Jewish scribe

CHAPTER 21

MATRIARCH IN MIAMI

"What a beautiful, open, and airy apartment," Rebbetzin Chani said.

"*Bruchim Ha'baim[1]*," Zina said warmly. The apartment was well-lit from the floor-to-ceiling windows, revealing a vivid life through the decor. Framed photos lined the living room and a long hall corridor; photographs of Zina and her family displayed lives that bounced out of their frames.

Zina gestured to a plate of dried fruit and nuts to offer her guest. "Please, help yourself."

As Chani dipped her fingers into the almond bowl, she noticed some photo albums on the coffee table.

"Each album is a travelogue. One of the cover albums is made from enamel with pearl chinoiserie, a remnant from my life in Asia."

---

1 *Bruchim Ha'baim (Hebrew)*– welcome

Zina flipped through one of the many albums where the tabs holding black and white photos in place were becoming loose and yellowing. "My children are urging me to do digital now."

"Oh, it is better this way. To hold in your hand what once was," Chani responded with comfort.

"I survived many challenges in my life. These are the treasures for my family," Zina said, selecting a plethora of photos to aid her in telling the stories of her parents, grandparents, and siblings, as well as the family she created with Yehuda, four children, and all her grandchildren.

Zina looked toward the framed photos, plaques, and artwork on her wall. With delicate fingers, she brushed over some dust on a plaque, admiring the memories cast on her wall:

Fundraising Excellence:
Sephardic Sisterhood Congregation of Queens 1979 - 1990

For Zina's dedicated service—
National Committee for Furtherance of Jewish Education
Life-Saving Work on Behalf of Iranian Children — Nov 1978

And then Zina touched matching plaques that had been awarded to her and Yehuda:

Profound Appreciation for Outstanding leadership for Israel—
1982 UJA, United Jewish Appeal

"Without Yehuda . . ." Zina looked away, cherishing her husband's memory. "This would not have been possible. After he passed in 2014, after our marriage of over fifty-five years, he left behind a huge legacy. He helped hundreds of people get settled in America, employed them, taught them his business—and he did it with a happiness felt by all."

Chani listened and nodded with admiration.

"Now my parents and in-laws are long gone, and my children have moved on to pursue their own lives and marriages: Gideon to Bangkok to further the gem business, Dahlia to Great Neck, Shirley to Manhattan, and Jackie is near me, here in Miami. My home is no longer the destination for visitors and extended family or Shabbat dinners. It's time for the next generation to take over."

"It does appear from all the photos you hosted hundreds of guests." Chani observed how Zina's life had changed.

"Our home was always full of food, family, and friends—then suddenly it felt like I was living in a mansion alone. I noticed with the passage of time in Forest Hills that what was once a strong Jewish—and Bukharan community—has decreased. Some friends passed away. Others had health problems or moved away. The community was changing. I chose to move to Miami. This way, I could continue living independently but with family nearby."

"That sounds like a community in change. It is so good you have some family here."

"And I'm so grateful for your weekly parsha studies that uplift me and connect me to my new community. I always try to extend the invitation to anyone who will benefit from your teachings."

"Thank you. Even though I have visited you before, I now grasp the whole story. I see family, laughter, joy, travel, flowing with the winds of history . . . you certainly have lived a full, blessed life."

"This is where I belong," Zina whispered. She had gathered these women together to prepare and cook food on this day—February 2, 2017. She spoke to the group with gratitude: "Thank you for coming to help cook the dishes for Bukharan night."

Several women responded, sharing that they were honored to learn to cook Bukharan foods. Together they made fragrant rice dishes and stuffed vegetables, naan bread, and salads.

"It is a remembrance of my childhood, where women had to support each other in all aspects of their lives as the men traveled the Silk Road. However, unlike my childhood, when meat was reserved only for holidays and festivals, we now have plenty of chicken and meat."

Cooking together in camaraderie was an expression of support for each other and Zina's communal history. The women talked about their traditions and several agreed that they were responsible for the physical survival of the family and culture—keeping the children fed, clothed, and safe—but also for the spiritual survival of the family and culture—preparing meals for holidays and passing on to their children, Jewish stories.

Soon the evening descended upon them, and the space filled up with guests dressed in bright and richly embroidered traditional dresses. Since Bukharan Night at the shul was an event spearheaded by Zina, it became a charity event celebrating sisterhood and survival. The event attracted more people than anyone anticipated.

String music and deep drums filled the evening; their enchantment only broke when Rebbetzin Chani introduced the guest speakers: Geula Sabet—a Sephardic historian and Bukharan public speaker—and Zina Abraham. Geula spoke of Bukharan history: the Silk Road and Jewish life in, at times, hostile Islamic countries. She recounted her own family history, as her story was parallel to Zina's.

"My grandfather, a rabbi descended from six generations of rabbis, was arrested by the Bolsheviks when he refused to stop teaching and practicing Judaism. When he managed to escape and hide with a Muslim family, his pregnant wife was arrested in his stead. In prison, she gave birth to twin boys. Both died of typhus."

Some women in the crowd gasped and solemnly shook their heads at the sadness of it all. "My grandfather, meanwhile, was smuggled into Iran, and by the time his wife was released from prison and able to join him, it was the late 1930s. After a few years in Tehran, the family moved to Jerusalem." Geula was born in pre-Independence Israel before moving with her family to New York in the 1950s.

When the Rebbetzin introduced Zina, the audience was primed with the history Geula provided and the knowledge that Geula and Zina's stories fed into each other: two stories of women's resilience, family ties, world travel, and Jewish pride.

Zina approached the low wooden podium, adjusting the microphone, and began to relate her family's history. "I will tell you the story of my parents, how my father was smuggled out of Russia, and how my mother was arrested for protecting him."

The audience immediately started murmuring. "I didn't know that!" whispered one of the women. Their disbelief would echo throughout Zina's story, until it evolved into admiration. It was hard for them to imagine that the speaker before them—the elegant, graceful woman who had led them in cooking and was a constant part of their sisterhood—was born into such a dangerous and unstable life.

No matter where Zina has lived or with whom she shared her living space, she has consistently built a home out of her will and spirit, out of her unbreakable focus on her loved ones and service to her community. Zina continued filling in the details of her tale: a twisting one of countries, family, perseverance, and adaptation, an exuberance of the human spirit. A Caravan of Hope.

"But first, you should know I was born in a Russian prison."

REFERENCES

Khan, Y. (2017). *The Great Partition: The Making of India and Pakistan.* Connecticut: Yale University Press, p.68

Koplik, S. (2015). *A Political and Economic History of the Jews of Afghanistan.* Netherlands: Brill Academic Publishing

Stronski, P. (2011). *Tashkent. Forging a Soviet City. 1930-1966.* Pennsylvania: University of Pittsburg Press

Acknowledgements

It takes a village to pull a book together such as this, with so many characters and many people no longer here with us. The first step to get this project off the ground was hiring Chey Wollner, who interviewed my mother, took videos, and copious notes on her life. When Covid hit, Chey face-timed my mother and continued to document her life. Thank you, Chey, for your years of working on this project.

I had the help of many writers to help me transform this transcript into its current form. Shannon Gonyou who was the first to generously offer her service to transform this into a living breathing story. My editor Katherine Factor who worked hours and hours to feel, breath and sense my family history and translate it into this book. Karen Offtitzer who offered suggestions on polishing up this manuscript towards the end. Debbie Manber Kupfer who went over and beyond proofreading into editing with such a keen and precise eye.

My great appreciation to Dan Shapira at Bar Ilan University who gleaned over this manuscript for accuracy.

Thank you to my family members who shared their stories with me, Moshe Abraham, Tamara Abraham, Yafa Bichoupan, Rosa Sharp, Davina Johnson, Shirley Abraham, and Liza Aronov. Your part of the family fabric led this book into its completion.

www.ingramcontent.com/pod-product-compliance
Lightning Source LLC
Chambersburg PA
CBHW020953160726
47994CB00006B/2201